HISTORY 1102
DEVELOPMENT OF
CONSTITUTIONAL GOVERNMENT

Although the colonists began the 1760s celebrating the accession of George III, they soon became disillusioned. Within a dozen years following the introduction of imperial reforms, the British colonists were in open rebellion against Great Britain. The sudden vehemence with which Americans moved into rebellion astonished their contemporaries as it has astonished historians ever since. A series of trade acts and tax levies did not seem to justify revolution. Yet by 1776 many Americans agreed with John Adams that the colonists were "in the very midst of a revolution, the most complete, unexpected and remarkable, of any in the history of nations." What could account for it? How was it to be justified?

The colonists admitted that it was not the particular acts of the British government that explained the Revolution; it was the meaning of those acts. Americans strove to understand the intentions of the British government and to determine their rights and liberties.

A military victory over Great Britain may have been a prerequisite for the success of the Revolution, but for Americans the Revolution meant more than simply eliminating a king and instituting an elective system of government. The Revolution was a moral upheaval that promised a fundamental shift in values and a change in the very character of American society. Originally designed to counter and reverse the modernizing tendencies of American life, republicanism ultimately quickened and magnified these trends.

In this unit you will look at the events that finally led to the Revolutionary War and at the kind of government that evolved in America. You will see the lives and events that molded the tenets of American government.

After establishing the English colonies in the New World, England left them alone for a time to do as they pleased. With the passage of the Navigation Acts in 1660, however, England's attitude toward the colonies changed, and she began to exploit the colonies by levying a variety of taxes to help fill her coffers. Another motive behind these taxes was the desire to bring the colonies under subjection.

The trade regulations England placed on the colonies led to colonial resistance in the New World. The greatest single reason for the tax increase was to finance the French and Indian War. The English thought that the colonies should pay for the war since the fighting had taken place in America, a sentiment that increased hard feelings among the colonies and led to still stronger resistance.

OBJECTIVES

Read these objectives. The objectives tell you what you should be able to do when you have successfully completed this LIFEPAC®.

When you have finished this LIFEPAC, you should be able to:

1. Name the various British actions regulating American trade.

2. Describe the events of the French and Indian War and its effect on colonial attitudes toward Britain.

3. Describe Britain's new policy restricting colonial freedoms and how it led to colonial resistance.

4. Describe the response of the colonists to Britain's actions.

5. Explain the Declaration of Independence.

6. Describe the strengths and weaknesses of the Continental army.

7. Describe the important events of the Revolutionary War.

8. Name people who contributed to the war.

9. Name the provisions of the Treaty of Paris of 1783.

10. State the strengths and weaknesses of the Articles of Confederation.
11. Describe the conflicting proposals of the Constitutional Convention.
12. Name the three branches of government and describe the system of checks and balances.
13. Explain the land ordinances of 1785 and 1787.
14. Describe the objections to and provisions of the Constitution.

Survey the LIFEPAC. Ask yourself some questions about this study. Write your questions here.

_____

_____

_____

_____

_____

_____

_____

_____

_____

_____

_____

I. RELATIONS WITH ENGLAND

SECTION OBJECTIVES

Review these objectives. When you have completed this section, you should be able to:

1. Name the various British actions regulating American trade.
2. Describe the events of the French and Indian War and its effect on colonial attitudes toward Britain.
3. Describe Britain's new policy restricting colonial freedoms and how it led to colonial resistance.

VOCABULARY

Study these words to enhance your learning success in this section.

boycott	To join together against and have nothing to do with (a person, business, nation, employer, or any other person or thing) in order to coerce or punish. If people are boycotting someone, they do not associate with him, or buy from or sell to him, and they try to keep others from doing so
mercantile theory	The economic system prevailing in Europe in the 1500s and 1600s which favored a balance of exports over imports, national wealth being measured by the amount of gold and silver possessed
treaty	An agreement, especially one between nations, signed and approved by each nation

Note: All vocabulary words in this LIFEPAC appear in **boldface** print the first time they are used. If you are unsure of the meaning when you are reading, study the definitions given.

HISTORY & GEOGRAPHY 1102
DEVELOPMENT OF CONSTITUTIONAL GOVERNMENT

CONTENTS

Author: Alpha Omega Staff
Editor: Alan Christopherson, M.S.
Illustrations: Alpha Omega Staff

Alpha Omega Publications®

804 N. 2nd Ave. E., Rock Rapids, IA 51246-1759
© MM by Alpha Omega Publications, Inc. All rights reserved.
LIFEPAC is a registered trademark of Alpha Omega Publications, Inc.

TRADE REGULATIONS

Trade is an important aspect of any country's economy. For England, the sea was a natural avenue of trade with other countries and with the colonies. Like other European nations, England at this time subscribed to the **mercantile theory**, which said that a country's power was measured by the amount of gold and silver it owned.

To strengthen her position as a world power, England passed the Navigation Acts in 1660, although the acts were not strictly enforced until the reign of George III. Later government regulations designed to take American merchants out of competition with the English included the Wool Act, the Hat Act, the Molasses Act, and the Sugar Act. Restrictions were placed on manufacture and the issuance of currency. Shortly before the French and Indian War, the writs of assistance were passed which allowed British officials to search colonists' homes.

Mercantilism. During the sixteenth century, England, France, Spain, Portugal, and Holland were engaged in a struggle for riches and power. Because the theory of mercantilism declared that the amount of gold and silver a country owned was more important than its military strength, each country wanted as large a supply of these metals as possible.

One method of securing gold was to have a colony trade only with the mother country. A colony would ship raw materials not available in the mother country, such as tobacco, naval stores, furs, and timber to the mother country. Manufacturers would then sell the goods they made from the raw materials back to the colonies. The colonies were prohibited from buying these goods from any other country. In this way the mother country was enriched, since the cost of the exported manufactured articles was higher than that of the imported raw materials. The difference in costs was paid in the important precious metals.

Mercantilism benefited the mother country, but not its colonies. As England passed more and stricter regulations to increase her own profit, the American colonists grew more and more disturbed.

Trade restrictions. English merchants did not want the Americans to compete with them in any way. When the colonists began to increase their production of wool to the point where the English wool raisers feared competition, the English Parliament passed the Wool Act of 1699. By this act all exports of wool products from any American colony to any other colony or to Europe were banned.

Bans were placed on other commodities as well. The growth in popularity of beaver hats and the existence of large numbers of these hats in America led to the Hat Act of 1732, which halted the export of beaver hats to Europe or to other colonies.

The Molasses Acts of 1733 and the Sugar Act of 1764 were passed to protect British West Indies planters from competition with the foreign West Indies islands. American shippers were forced to accept these measures because they had built up a profitable trade with the French and the Dutch, paying lower prices to them than those charged by the English.

Manufacturing restrictions. Trade was not the only aspect of the American economy restricted by the English. Industry and manufacturing in the colonies were also limited. The Hat Act of 1732 affected the American hat industry. To prevent further growth of the iron industry in the colonies, the Iron Act of 1759 prohibited the building of iron mills and steel furnaces, at the same time encouraged the production of raw iron by allowing it to enter England duty-free.

Currency control. Another method the English used to hold back economic growth was to control currency. The amount of money in the colonies was never enough to meet the needs of the colonies. The shortage of actual currency led many colonists to adopt a system of barter. Under this system a raw material such as wool could be exchanged for shoes, rice, or wheat.

Navigation Acts. Beginning in 1660, England passed a series of laws called the Navigation Acts. These acts controlled all colonial trade. The first Navigation Act required that all ships carrying goods between England and America be English-built or owned. Certain articles which included tobacco, sugar, indigo, and naval stores, could be sold only to England.

The Navigation Acts were later extended to include molasses, beaver skins, and other furs. The English government intended that these laws reduce the growing strength of the colonies. However, they did not cause friction with the colonists because they were loosely enforced.

The reason for lax enforcement was that the English were busy with affairs of the empire between 1685 and 1763, when they were fighting a series of wars with France. The English hoped to keep the colonies loyal to her by not enforcing these laws too strictly, in case the French in the New World declared war.

Another reason was the conflict between the king and the Parliament. The Puritan Revolution of 1689 forced the English government to neglect the colonies. Officials, too, were not eager to carry out the laws because growing trade and commerce between England and the colonies provided more profits to British merchants.

Also, because of geographical considerations, strict enforcement would have required many more ships than England had available. There was a great distance between England and the colonies, and the American coastline was long and irregular. The many harbors encouraged smuggling by the colonists to evade the laws and import or export goods illegally.

England decided to enforce the Navigation Acts after 1763. England's troubles at home were settled when a new king, George III, came to the throne. Since France had been pushed from the North American continent as a result of the French and Indian War, England could now pay more attention to the colonies. The English government had spent large sums of money in this war and, since the colonies had benefited from it, the English felt that the colonists should pay part of the cost.

Writs of assistance. Before the French and Indian War ended, the government had decided on a new policy toward the colonies. In 1761 the British officials were ordered to enforce the Navigation Acts more strictly and to seize all goods smuggled into the colonies. The officials were given the power to use legal papers called *writs of assistance* to enter the warehouses, shops, and homes of the colonists to look for smuggled goods.

These *writs of assistance* created a great deal of concern in the colonies since they gave British officials the right to enter at will and confiscate anything that the owner was unable to prove was not smuggled. A Boston lawyer, James Otis, protested that the *writs of assistance* violated one of the basic liberties of Englishmen, freedom from unreasonable search. Otis charged that the writs did not specify any particular place to search but were so general in nature that no colonial home was safe. However, Otis lost the case and the writs continued to be used.

Match these items with correct descriptions.

1.1 _____ first Navigation Act   a. allowed raw iron to enter England duty free

1.2 _____ Iron Act   b. allowed the British to search homes

1.3 _____ writs of assistance   c. prevent competition with foreign West Indies islands

1.4 _____ Molasses Act   d. only English ships could be used

1.5 _____ Hat Act   e. used by the colonists because of a currency shortage

1.6 _____ barter   f. prevented manufacturing and competition in 1732

True/False.

1.7 _____ The Navigation Acts were intended to strengthen the shaky economy of the colonies.

1.8 _____ The Navigation Acts began to be strictly enforced during the time of George III.

Fill in the blanks.

1.9 The _____ theory stated that a country's power was measured by the amount of gold and silver it owned.

1.10 The Boston lawyer who unsuccessfully tried to have the writs of assistance removed was

_____ .

1.11 Name four articles that could be sold only to England because of the Navigation Acts.

a. _____ ,   b. _____ ,

c. _____ ,   d. _____ .

1.12 Name three additional acts that placed government regulations on trade.

a. _____ ,

b. _____ ,

c. _____ .

Answer the question.

1.13 How did the economic system of the colonies benefit England?

_____

_____

_____

_____

_____

FRENCH AND INDIAN WAR

Although Spain had claimed a large part of the North American continent, control in the north was largely divided between the English and the French. The French had explored and colonized Canada, the Ohio Valley, and the Mississippi Valley before the English had arrived; but their colonies had never grown very large.

Because of the differences in government, economy, population, and Indian relations, war seemed inevitable. England and France had fought three wars in Europe over a period of seventy-five years; now it was time to fight a colonial war in America. Each country wanted to control the new land. Central to that control was power over the rich Ohio Valley Territory, where the war would begin.

Because of the increasing French presence in America, the English colonists called the Albany Congress to encourage the colonies to band together as one unit to resist the French. War began in 1755 with the defeat of General Braddock in the Ohio Valley and then moved on to New York. Finally, the Battle of Quebec in 1759 resulted in the defeat of the French in North America.

In 1763 the **Treaty** of Paris was signed, bringing an end to the war and permitting the English to gain control of North America.

English and French colonial differences. The French and the English held prominent positions among world powers. The involvement of both countries in the colonies led to many conflicts. Each country wanted to dominate the colonies; neither would tolerate the other's presence there. The extreme differences between the two countries in their approaches and in their positions in the colonies, created friction.

The French colonies sprawled over a vast area of North America—from the Mississippi River Valley in the heart of the continent, along the Great Lakes to eastern Canada and the St. Lawrence River, and westward through the countryside to the Allegheny and Appalachian mountain ranges.

The English colonies spanned most of the coast of North America. In 1760 the French empire had a population of about 80,000 colonists spread out among sparsely populated settlements. Only three major towns were in the French empire in North America: New Orleans, Quebec, and Montreal. About 15 percent of the French people lived in these towns. The rest were trappers, traders, missionaries, and settlers living in small outposts or traveling around the vast French empire.

In contrast, the English colonists numbered a little more than 1.5 million in 1760. The majority of the colonists lived in towns of fair size or in fine cities. The largest city was Boston, with 42,000 inhabitants.

The French did not try to develop the resources of their empire. For them, the chief value of the colonies was the fur trade. Many Frenchmen trapped animals for furs or traded with the Indians. Some farming was carried on in the St. Lawrence Valley, but it was not very important economically.

Most English colonists, however, became permanent settlers. They built houses, farmed the land, and used the available resources of the country. Building ships, growing wheat, lumbering, cultivating tobacco, rice, indigo, and trapping for fur were only some of the occupations found in the English colonies.

The French never developed a system of representative government. All power was in the hands of the royal governor. The people had no particular voice in the laws drawn up by the king or his representatives, nor was there any religious freedom for non-Catholics in New France.

The English colonists developed representative government early through their charters and elected assemblies. Such bodies had the right to make laws and to levy taxes. More religious liberty was to be found in the English colonies than in the French. When the French Protestants left France, they did not settle in Canada, but in the English colonies where they were allowed the religious freedom denied to them in France.

One advantage the French had over the English was that their government was in the hands of one person and decisions could be made more quickly than in the thirteen English colonies.

A second advantage held by the French was the friendly relationship they had established with most of the Indian tribes living in the rival empire. Friendly relations with the Indians were an economic necessity for the French, since they depended upon the Indians for furs. The Indians were less friendly with the English. Many tribes hated the English for driving them from their homes and land. The one exception was the Iroquois tribes of New York, whose hatred for the French was based on the support given by the explorer Champlain to the Algonquian Indians during a war between the two tribes more than one hundred years before.

English and French colonial wars. England and France fought a series of wars lasting over a period of seventy-five years. The first three wars had very little effect on the possessions of both countries in the New World. The fourth war, called the French and Indian War (1756-1763), drove out the French from the mainland of the North American continent.

The first clash between the French and the English in the New World was King George's War, begun in 1745. The French seized the prosperous sugar island of St. Lucia in the West Indies; and the British, with the aid of their colonies, captured Louisbourg on Cape Breton Island.

When the war ended in a draw in 1748, the peace treaty provided that the land captured by both sides during the fighting had to be returned to its original owners. The English returned Cape Breton to the French, but the French remained in St. Lucia. This treachery became one more area of contention between the French and the English.

England tried to negotiate a settlement for the return of St. Lucia. The French responded by complaining about England's aggression in other places, especially the building of an English stronghold in Nova Scotia.

The French began winning several of the important Indian tribes over to their side by telling them that they would protect them from the English. To show that they meant what they said, they began to build forts in key areas where there might be possible conflict with the English. However, the English responded by building forts of their own.

Ohio Valley conflict. Both the French and the English considered the Ohio Valley to be the most valuable possession of all. The problem began in 1749 when some Virginia promoters encouraged settlers to go into the Ohio River Valley. The promoters had obtained a grant of thousands of acres of land from the English king for their venture. Before long, a stream of frontiersmen from Virginia was moving steadily into the Ohio Valley. The new governor of New France, Marquis Duquesne, was so angered by this intrusion that he decided to construct a series of forts from Lake Erie to the Ohio River to halt the flow of frontiersmen.

The concern felt in Virginia was immediate. Robert Dinwiddie, the lieutenant governor, was especially interested because of his investments in the Ohio Company and did not hesitate to take action. In 1753 he sent a young man named George Washington to Fort Venango to try to persuade the French to leave English (Virginian) soil. Washington was received cordially. The French, however, were determined to have all of the Ohio Valley as their own without interference from anyone else.

Lieutenant Governor Dinwiddie decided to build a fort where the Ohio River met the Allegheny and the Monongahela rivers. In early 1754, a small army led by Washington set out to build the fort. Washington learned that the French were constructing Fort Duquesne at the same place. Instead of returning to Virginia, Washington decided to go against the French with his small band of 150 men. Washington encountered and defeated a small party of French soldiers. Knowing that the French would soon come after him, he ordered his men to establish a fort as quickly as possible. The stronghold was aptly named Fort Necessity. The French soon found Washington and his men. Fort Necessity was no match for the large French army, and Washington was soon defeated. He returned to Virginia with the remainder of his army, having fought the opening battle of the French and Indian War.

English Albany Plan. The English officials, realizing that the defense against the French would be strengthened by a union of the colonies, called a meeting at Albany. Seven of the thirteen colonies sent representatives. Benjamin Franklin, the delegate from Pennsylvania, proposed that all the colonies band together in a union. A legislature would be formed that would consist of a president general, to be appointed by the king, and a council, whose members would be chosen by the colonial legislatures. This legislature would represent all the colonies. The legislature would also have control over Indian affairs and would build an army for the defense of all the colonies, both subject to the approval of the president general and the crown.

The colonies did not accept the Albany Plan of Union, refusing to give up any of their own powers to one central authority. The English also turned down the plan because they preferred to deal with the colonies individually rather than as a group.

Braddock's campaign. The English sent over an army of British regulars under the leadership of General Edward Braddock. These two regiments were responsible for removing the French from the Ohio Valley. Braddock was severely handicapped by his lack of understanding of Indian fighting methods. When he led the troops that attacked Fort Duquesne, Braddock sent 300 axmen ahead of him to clear a way through the forest. With his army of 1,400 regulars and 450 Virginia militiamen under Washington, Braddock pushed forward toward Fort Duquesne. On July 9, 1755, Braddock's army was soundly defeated when it was met by an advance force of French and Indians. Braddock and most of his 1,400 regulars were killed. Washington and the remainder of the Virginia militia returned safely to Virginia.

In New York Colonel William Johnson, a friend of the Iroquois, won their aid against the French. He defeated the French at Lake George, and thus ended the French efforts to gain control of New York.

In 1759 the English sent out large forces. A drive in western and northern New York won Fort Niagara, Ticonderoga, and Crown Point. An English fleet carrying troops under the command of General James Wolfe sailed up the St. Lawrence River and besieged the city of Quebec, located on top of an extremely high bluff. In a surprise move, General Wolfe

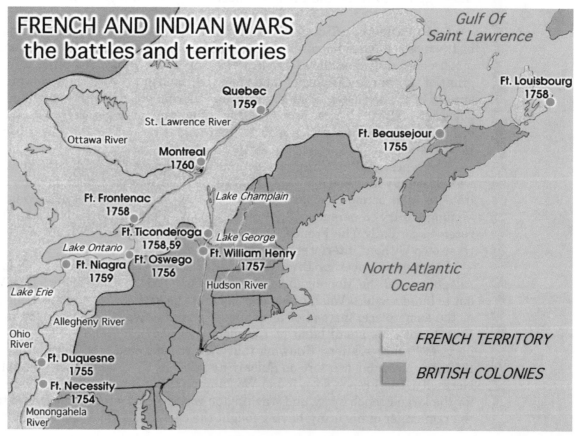

8

led his soldiers up the side of the bluff during the night and at dawn had his army ready for attack on the Plains of Abraham behind the city. Both commanders, General Wolfe of England and General Marquis de Montcalm of France, were killed in the ensuing fighting. The English won the battle and a few days later Quebec surrendered to the English.

During 1760 Montreal, Detroit, and other French forts along the Great Lakes were captured by the English, ending the French empire in North America.

Treaty of Paris, 1763. The Treaty of Paris in 1763 ended the French and Indian War. While fighting continued in the New World, the French and English were also fighting in Europe. The peace treaty that was drawn up reflected the great triumph that England enjoyed throughout every part of the world. France lost almost all its possessions and foreign trade.

In America, England acquired Canada and France's territory east of the Mississippi, except for New Orleans. The islands of Martinique and Guadeloupe, which were important sugar-producing islands in the West Indies, and Haiti, half of the island of Hispaniola, were returned to France. The English gave Cuba and the Philippines back to Spain and received Florida in return.

Having persuaded Spain to enter the war in what was a hopeless cause for them, France gave Spain New Orleans and all the land it claimed west of the Mississippi River. France received fishing privileges off the coast of Newfoundland and the islands of St. Pierre and Miquelon.

The defeat of the French and the acquisition of new territory made England the leading colonial power in the world. To help pay the costs of the war, however, England had to increase revenues from the colonies and make them pay for the victory they had won. This victory also gave England more opportunity to concentrate on the colonies, now that France was no longer a threat.

To the colonists, the elimination of the French brought a welcome relief. They no longer needed to look to England for protection against the French. The colonists had gained valuable military experience and now knew their own strength. The result of all these factors was a change in the relations between the mother country and the colonies; no longer were they so dependent. The events of these early years were shaping the future of the colonies into that of an ultimately great nation.

AMERICA IN 1763

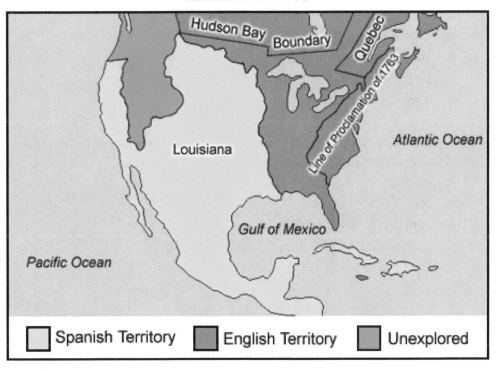

Spanish Territory · English Territory · Unexplored

Write the letter of the correct answer on the line.

1.14   The French and Indian War broke out over claims to the _____ .
    a. Mississippi River Valley
    b. Ohio River Valley
    c. Mohawk River Valley
    d. Hudson River Valley

1.15   One of the deciding battles of the French and Indian War was the capture of Quebec by General _____ .
    a. Montcalm
    b. Braddock
    c. Washington
    d. Wolfe

1.16   As a result of the treaty of Paris of 1763, the French ceded _____ .
    a. New Orleans to the English
    b. territory west of the Mississippi to the English
    c. Canada and the area east of the Mississippi to the English
    d. Louisiana to the English

1.17   One result of the French and Indian War was that England _____ .
    a. reduced colonial taxes
    b. wanted the colonies to help pay for the war
    c. gave the colonies their freedom
    d. erased all colonial dissatisfactions

1.18   The Albany Plan of Union was drawn up by _____ .
    a. Samuel Adams
    b. Benjamin Franklin
    c. George Washington
    d. Thomas Jefferson

1.19   General Braddock's greatest weakness in the French and Indian War was his lack of _____ .
    a. courage
    b. control over his men
    c. support by the British
    d. understanding of Indian fighting methods

1.20   The final American war between France and England was _____ .
        a. King William's War
        b. the French and Indian War
        c. King George's War
        d. Queen Anne's War

1.21   The Albany Plan of Union was proposed in order to _____ .
        a. secure foreign allies for the colonies
        b. fight for independence
        c. strengthen the colonies against the French
        d. defy the English trade restrictions

Complete the following statements.

1.22   Most of the French settlers trapped _____ and
        traded with the _____ .

1.23   England's Indian allies were the _____ .

1.24   General Braddock and George Washington led an attack against the French
        at Fort _____ .

COLONIAL RESISTANCE

The French and Indian War had been expensive for the British government, costing approximately $350,000,000. Since the American colonists had benefited most from the war, the British felt that the colonies should help pay the war debt. Their attitude was that more money could be raised by a stricter enforcement of the Navigation Acts. King George III of England also felt that the colonies were too independent of England. He wanted to bring them under more direct and strict control by his government. For these reasons, a new colonial policy restricting colonial freedoms was carried out by the British.

The Proclamation Act of 1763. The first move was the Proclamation Act of 1763, which closed the newly acquired lands west of the Allegheny Mountains to American trappers and settlers. The English wanted the Americans to remain along the Atlantic coast, partly because they could be controlled more easily there and also because they wanted to avoid trouble with the Indians. This order angered the colonists, who felt these western lands belonged to them.

The Grenville Program. To raise more money in the colonies, the Chancellor of the Exchequer, Lord Grenville, ordered an increase in old taxes and the levying of some new ones on many imported goods coming into the colonies. To enforce these new taxes, the Quartering Act provided for 10,000 British troops to be stationed, fed, and housed in America by the colonists.

The Stamp Act. The first direct tax levied by England on the colonists was the Stamp Tax. The Stamp Act of 1765 placed a tax on paper materials used in the colonies, including all newspapers, pamphlets, and legal documents, as well as calendars and playing cards. Because of the tax, fires were set, riots broke out, and debates took place in the colonial assemblies.

In the Virginia House of Burgesses, Patrick Henry warned the king of England of the possible effects of such a law. Several of the members accused Henry of treason, to which he replied, "If this be treason, make the most of it." The House of Burgesses drew up the Virginia Resolves condemning the Stamp Act and maintaining that only the colonial governments had the right to levy taxes.

The Sons of Liberty. Opposition to the tax was led by a secret organization called the Sons of Liberty, whose members included some of the leading citizens in the colonies, among them Paul Revere of Massachusetts. Deciding that the Stamp Tax should not be paid, the Sons of Liberty staged parades and protests, destroyed the stamps, and drove out the stamp distributors. The Sons of Liberty also enforced an unofficial **boycott** of English goods.

The Stamp Act Congress. In 1765 representatives from nine colonies met in New York to draw up a protest against the hated Stamp Tax. Led by John Dickinson of Pennsylvania, the delegates drew up a "Declaration of Rights and Grievances" stating their loyalty to the British government but protesting the tax. The representatives claimed that they were entitled to all the rights and liberties of Englishmen including the right to tax themselves through their elected representatives.

When the British exports to America declined as a result of the boycott and opposition to the tax, the British Parliament repealed the Stamp Tax. At the same time, however, it passed a Declaratory Law which allowed Parliament to pass any laws on any matter in the colonies.

The Townshend Program. The new Chancellor of the Exchequer, Charles Townshend, proposed a new series of taxes to increase English revenues from the colonies. Taxes were to be levied on lead, glass, paper, paint, and tea. Part of the money raised from those new taxes was to pay the salaries of the officials who were enforcing the law. Until that time colonial assemblies had paid those officers, but the new law severely weakened colonial control over them.

To eliminate smuggling, the officials were given writs of assistance to enter many places to search for and seize any goods that had come into the colonies illegally. Colonists accused of violating the laws were to be tried without a jury and punished. Any appeals from these trials were to be taken to England.

The Colonial Reactions. The colonists reacted by boycotting English goods. During the next two years, more and more merchants refused to buy English products, and the people fully supported them in the boycott. Because the boycott spread through the colonies, the sale of English products fell almost 50 percent. Because the Sons of Liberty were gaining popular support, the British sent troops to Boston to maintain order.

In 1770 the British merchants complained to the Parliament about the severe loss of business. Parliament listened to the merchants and repealed all of the taxes except the tax on tea, which remained as proof to the colonies that Parliament still had the power to tax them. This intentional oversight did not bother the colonists very much, since smuggled tea was cheaper than English tea.

The Boston Massacre. Meanwhile, the British troops that were stationed in Boston were encountering problems with the local citizens. The problems persisted until a riot broke out in March of 1770 between a group of soldiers and the town workers. As the riot spread, additional soldiers were called out and some of them fired into the crowd, killing five people and wounding several others. This incident, called the Boston Massacre, increased the hatred against the British that was growing in the colonies.

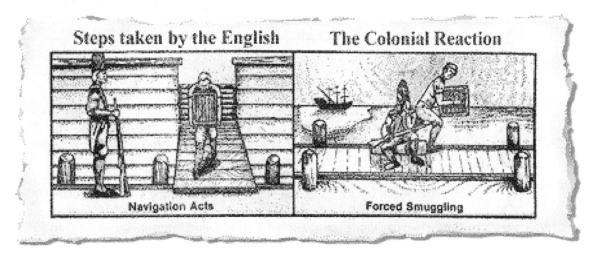

Steps taken by the English — Navigation Acts

The Colonial Reaction — Forced Smuggling

Steps taken by the English — Stamp Act

The Colonial Reaction — Fires, Riots Break Out

Steps taken by the English — Townshend Program

The Colonial Reaction — Virginia Resolves

Steps taken by the English — The Tea Tax

The Colonial Reaction — Boston Tea Party

The Committees of Correspondence. The lack of communication was a serious problem for the colonists. Under the inspiring leadership of Samuel Adams, a Committee of Correspondence consisting of twenty-one men was formed in Massachusetts to keep in touch with similar committees in the other colonies. A chain of communication was formed with the other colonies by sending fast riders with the news. Samuel Adams was the man most responsible for keeping the committees in touch with each other.

The Boston Tea Party. Tempers flared and emotions took over in 1773. When the East India Company faced near bankruptcy, George III gave it the right to sell tea to the American colonists at a lower price than smuggled tea. Many colonists opposed this move, fearing that it would hurt the colonial tea business. The company sent out ships loaded with tea to Philadelphia, New York, and Boston. The officials at Philadelphia and New York refused to allow the ships to dock in their harbors, but the governor of Massachusetts allowed the ship to dock at Boston harbor. The colonists were so infuriated by this decision that they dressed as Indians, boarded the ship, and threw the tea into the harbor.

The Intolerable Acts. In order to punish the colonists for destroying the tea, the British Parliament passed a series of acts against the city of Boston. Because these acts were so harsh, the colonists referred to them as the Intolerable Acts. The port of Boston was closed, with no ships allowed to enter or leave the harbor until the tea was paid for. The charter (constitution) of Massachusetts was taken away from the colony. Town meetings were not permitted without the consent of the governor. All officials were to be appointed by the governor. More British troops were moved into Boston and stationed in the houses of the colonists. British officers and soldiers who were accused of crimes against colonists were to be tried in England, not in the colony where the crime was committed. The Northwest Territory, which was partly claimed by Massachusetts, was annexed by Quebec. Since these acts adversely affected all the colonies, not just Massachusetts, they served to unite the colonies against the British.

The First Continental Congress. A movement spread among the colonies to call a general congress represented by delegates from all the colonies. The delegates would decide what steps should be taken in overcoming the problems with the British government. In early September of 1774, fifty-six delegates from twelve colonies met at Philadelphia particularly in response to the Intolerable Acts. Many of the leading figures of the Revolution were present, including Samuel Adams and John Adams of Massachusetts, Patrick Henry and Richard Henry Lee of Virginia, and Joseph Galloway of Pennsylvania.

After lengthy debates, the First Continental Congress drew up a Declaration of Rights and Grievances which openly denounced the Intolerable Acts as being unjust and unconstitutional. They also drew up a list of colonial rights: life, liberty, property ownership, the control of taxation by the colonial legislatures, and others.

The delegates agreed to organize an American association that would buy no goods from England until the Intolerable Acts had been repealed by the British government. The congress also urged the Americans to arm themselves. It was hoped that the petition would lead the king to settle the dispute. In the meantime, the congress adjourned until the following May, agreeing to meet only if the colonial grievances were not settled.

All of these events were building toward a climax of war with the British. The arrest of Samuel Adams and John Hancock had been ordered by the British, an event which resulted in the famous rides of Paul Revere and William Dawes. The battles of Lexington and Concord were fought a few days later. On May 10, 1775, the Second Continental Congress met and organized an army with George Washington as the commander-in-chief. The war had begun, and the British would have to fight hard if they were to hold the colonies. Thus, the growing spirit for independence had led to the beginning of the Revolutionary War.

Complete the following statement.

1.25   To join together against and have nothing to do with a person, business, nation, employer, or

any other person or thing in order to coerce or punish is called a _____ .

Match each word with its correct definition.

1.26   _____ Proclamation Act of 1763   a. troops were stationed in colonial homes

1.27   _____ Quartering Act   b. prohibited settlers from moving west

1.28   _____ Virginia Resolves   c. secret organizations opposed to the stamp tax

1.29   _____ Committees of Correspondence   d. a chain of communication with other colonies

1.30   _____ Sons of Liberty   e. result of Stamp Act

1.31   _____ writ of assistance   f. Parliament allowed to pass any laws

1.32   _____ Declaratory Law   g. allowed the British to search colonists' homes

Write the letter of the correct answer on the line.

1.33   The Stamp Act forced the colonists to pay a tax on _____ .

    a. tea

    b. paper

    c. sugar

    d. coffee

1.34   Passage of the Townshend Acts caused the colonists to _____ .

    a. revolt

    b. urge Congress to veto the Act

    c. boycott English goods

    d. go on a hunger strike

1.35   The Committees of Correspondence were organized by _____ .

    a. Samuel Adams

    b. James Otis

    c. Patrick Henry

    d. Paul Revere

1.36   The Boston Tea Party was _____ .

    a. a celebration of the harvest of tea leaves

    b. an annual social event

    c. a protest against the tea drinkers of Boston

    d. a protest against the tea tax

1.37   The Intolerable Acts caused the formation of _____ .

    a. political parties

    b. the Minutemen

    c. a continental army

    d. a continental navy

Adult Check   _____

                    Initial   **Date**

Review the material in this section in preparation for the Self Test. The Self Test will checkyour mastery of this particular section. The items missed on this Self Test will indicate specific areas where restudy is needed for mastery.

SELF TEST I

Answer *true* **or** *false* (each answer, 1 point).

1.01 _____ The colonists called the Albany Congress to encourage unity.

1.02 _____ Lieutenant Governor Dinwiddie was known for his defeat of the French at Quebec.

1.03 _____ The French and Indian War was the final American war between France and England.

1.04 _____ From their beginning, the Navigation Acts were strictly enforced.

1.05 _____ The shortage of money in the colonies forced the colonists to use a barter system.

1.06 _____ The Revolution was not caused so much by the acts of the British government as by their attitudes.

Match each word to its correct description (each answer, 2 points).

1.07 _____ Virginia   a. Intolerable Acts

1.08 _____ Fort Necessity   b. George Washington

1.09 _____ Boston   c. Lieutenant Governor Dinwiddie

1.010 _____ Sam Adams   d. First Continental Congress

1.011 _____ 1774   e. Committees of Correspondence

Fill in the blanks (each answer, 3 points).

1.012 The Intolerable Acts were passed to punish Boston for the _____.

1.013 In protest of the Stamp Act, a group called the _____ boycotted English goods.

1.014 The idea that the power of a country is measured in terms of its gold and silver is called _____ theory.

1.015 The First Continental Congress drew up a Declaration of _____.

1.016 The Boston lawyer who opposed the writs of assistance was _____.

1.017 The _____ program levied taxes to pay the salaries of those enforcing the law.

1.018 Name five acts or taxes that controlled trade of specific items.
a. _____ , b. _____ , c. _____ ,
d. _____ , e. _____ .

1.019 The _____ met to react to the Intolerable Acts and decide steps to be taken in the conflict with Britain.

Place a check beside the four correct answers (each answer, 2 points).

1.020 Why were the Navigation Acts not initially enforced by England?

_____ a. Raw iron from the colonies was being imported to England duty-free.

_____ b. England was at war with France and wanted the loyalty of the colonies.

_____ c. The colonies were growing in strength.

_____ d. American merchants were competing with English merchants.

_____ e. A struggle was going on between the king of England and Parliament.

_____ f. Growing trade with the colonies gave more profits to the British.

_____ g. A great distance separated England and the colonies.

_____ h. The colonists followed the laws of the Navigation Acts.

17

Write the letter of the correct answer on the line (each answer, 2 points).

1.021   The regulation that permitted the English to search colonial homes was _____ .
    a. the Intolerable Acts
    b. the Import-Export Act
    c. the writs of assistance
    d. the Albany Plan

1.022   The Treaty of Paris, 1763, returned _____ .
    a. Martinique to France
    b. Guadeloupe to France
    c. Haiti to France
    d. all of the above

1.023   Lord Grenville's program included the _____ .
    a. Proclamation Act
    b. Quartering Act
    c. Stamp Act
    d. Virginia Resolves

1.024   The man who said, "If this be treason, make the most of it," was _____ .
    a. George Washington
    b. Samuel Adams
    c. Benjamin Franklin
    d. Patrick Henry

1.025   The order to arrest two men resulted in the rides of Paul Revere and William Dawes.
Which two men were to be arrested? _____ and _____ .
    a. Patrick Henry
    b. Samuel Adams
    c. John Hancock
    d. James Otis
    e. John Adams

Number the following events in proper sequence 1–5 (each answer, 2 points).

1.026   _____   the Committees of Correspondence
1.027   _____   the Boston Tea Party
1.028   _____   the Stamp Act
1.029   _____   the Intolerable Acts
1.030   _____   French and Indian War

66 / 82

II. THE REVOLUTIONARY WAR

"The battle, sir, is not to the strong alone; it is to the vigilant, the active, the brave...If we were base enough to desire it, it is now too late to retire from the contest. There is no retreat but in submission and slavery! Our chains are forged. Their clanking may be heard upon the plains of Boston! The war is inevitable—and let it come! I repeat, sir, let it come!" At the Virginia convention to choose delegates to a Second Continental Congress, the eloquent Patrick Henry prophesied that the Congress would do far more than strike back at the British for the clash at Lexington and Concord. Before the congress adjourned, it would conduct a long and bitter war for independence from Great Britain.

On the face of it, such a war seemed preposterous. The colonies were economically weak and politically inexperienced. Moreover, they did not even have a regular army until the Second Continental Congress authorized the raising of troops in 1775. Great Britain, on the other hand, was a leading world power.

Nevertheless, the American colonies eventually secured their freedom. Among the factors contributing to their victory were the persistence of Patriot colonists, the inspiring leadership of George Washington and the generous aid of the French. How these forces combined to win the independence of the United States is the next part of the unfolding story of America.

SECTION OBJECTIVES

Review these objectives. When you have completed this section, you should be able to:

4. Describe the response of the colonists to Britain's actions.
5. Explain the Declaration of Independence.
6. Describe the strengths and weaknesses of the Continental army.
7. Describe the important events of the Revolutionary War.
8. Name people who contributed to the war.

VOCABULARY

Study these words to enhance your learning success in this section.

compromise	To settle (a quarrel or difference of opinion) by agreeing that each will give up a part of what he demands; come to terms
mercenary	A soldier hired for pay by a foreign state
ally	A person, group, or nation united with another for some special purpose
Loyalist	An American colonist who opposed independence for the American colonies at the time of Revolutionary War; a Tory
treaty	An agreement, especially one between nations, signed and approved by each nation
privateer	An armed ship owned by private persons and holding a government commission to attack and capture enemy vessels

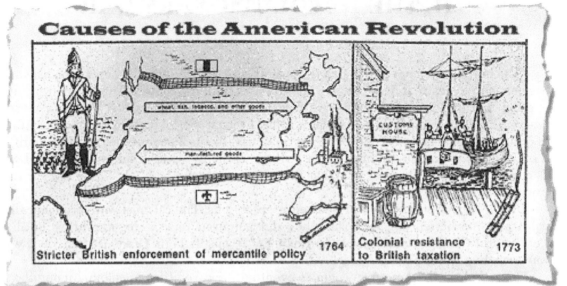

Causes of the American Revolution

Stricter British enforcement of mercantile policy — 1764

Colonial resistance to British taxation — 1773

Causes of the American Revolution

Royal decree preventing sale of western land — 1763

Opposition to keeping a British army in America — 1774

Weakening of ties through space and time

Causes of the American Revolution

Struggle for more colonial home rule

Many skilled colonial leaders emerge

AMERICAN REVOLUTION — 1775

SECOND CONTINENTAL CONGRESS

Before adjourning, the First Continental Congress had made plans to reconvene if the grievances against England had not been solved. The news of the fighting at Lexington and Concord in Massachusetts greeted the delegates as they assembled in Philadelphia for the Second Continental Congress in May of 1775.

A few of the delegates still hoped to patch up the differences between the colonies and England, but the majority had come to believe that only a show of armed strength by the Americans could win concessions. The Patriots felt that England would never come to terms now that the colonists had dared to fight against them. They believed that only complete independence could resolve the difficulties.

Decisive action taken. The first problem confronting the congress involved Massachusetts. After halting the British advance, the Minutemen had driven them back into Boston. The Massachusetts militia was growing rapidly. Congress decided to establish a Continental Army with the militia from Massachusetts as part of it. George Washington, well known as a leader in the French and Indian War, a respected member of the Virginia House of Burgesses, and a staunch supporter of colonial causes, was chosen commander-in-chief. He helped the Patriots to persist in what often seemed to be a hopeless cause. Without Washington, independence might not have been achieved.

For the congress to choose Washington to lead the army was easy enough, but for the congress to decide on their policy toward Britain was far more difficult. Finally, in July of 1775, the congress adopted a "Declaration of the Causes and Necessity of Taking up Arms" explaining to the king and to Parliament the reasons the colonists were fighting the British in Boston. Near the end of the series of meetings, congress insisted that they did not mean to dissolve the union that had existed so long. The congress endorsed the Olive Branch Petition begging Parliament to wait until an understanding could be achieved.

If the British government had accepted the *Olive Branch Petition,* discussions might have led to a **compromise**. However, the king angrily rejected the petition on the grounds that it was issued by assembly. The king immediately approved an act prohibiting all trade with the colonies and sent 30,000 troops as well as foreign **mercenaries** to crush the rebellion. Many of the foreign mercenaries were German soldiers called Hessians. Benjamin Franklin pointed out the irony in the British government's paying German soldiers to kill American colonists. Throughout the war, the presence of Hessians stirred the colonists to greater resistance.

In Massachusetts, the Patriot recruits gathered in towns surrounding Boston. Although they were armed, the Patriots had little training and no uniforms. These men did have the courage to face the highly trained British troops that were assembled in Boston. During the night of June 16, 1775, approximately twelve hundred Patriots climbed Bunker Hill and Breed's Hill overlooking the city of Boston. Their plan was to hold these hills and to force the British to leave Boston.

When morning came, the astonished British found that the Americans had taken up positions on Breed's Hill. General Gage, commander of the British redcoats, sent a body of troops to drive the Americans from their strategic location. While the citizens of Boston watched intently from their housetops, lines of British troops advanced in perfect order toward the summit of the hill. On two occasions they nearly reached the top, only to be driven back by the sharp-shooting Patriots. Since the Patriots were running short of powder, they were forced to withdraw from the hill when the British attacked for the third time.

The British, who felt that their troops were the finest in the world, were faced by untrained Patriots in the Battle of Bunker Hill, yet they suffered almost double the losses that the Patriots sustained. During the ensuing months, the Patriot forces continued to surround Boston but were unable to clear the city of British troops.

Early in 1776, the Patriots dragged cannons hundreds of miles overland from northeastern New York to Boston and placed them on a strategic hill overlooking the Boston harbor. General Howe, the British commander, decided that Boston could no longer be held and ordered the British troops removed to Halifax, Nova Scotia. The Patriots entered Boston and held it. No other major battles were fought in New England during the Revolutionary War.

While the battle was going on in the Boston area, Ethan Allan and other Patriots seized Fort Ticonderoga in northeastern New York. The British also lost the battle at Crown Point.

These two victories encouraged the colonists to invade Canada and to seize Montreal. However, another expedition failed to take Quebec. In time, both expeditions withdrew because the combined forces of Benedict Arnold and General Richard Montgomery failed to capture Quebec. Arnold was wounded and Montgomery was killed in the disastrous battle. After a starving winter outside Quebec, the colonists retreated to Fort Ticonderoga when British reinforcements arrived in the spring.

In the Carolinas, more fighting was taking place. The North Carolina Patriots defeated a group of colonists who had taken the side of the British. A British attack on Charleston was also successfully turned back.

During this period many of the colonists still hoped for a reconciliation with England. The colonists believed that their efforts and willingness to shed their own blood would show the British leaders that they were bitterly opposed to the strict control from England and that a more lenient attitude should be taken by the British leaders. However, instead of adopting a gentler approach, the British leaders declared that if the colonists rebelled the British would establish a still harsher policy.

The most stirring argument for independence came from the writings of Thomas Paine, who had recently come to America from England. In his pamphlet, "Common Sense," he called upon the Americans to break away from Great Britain. The break, he argued, was only common sense. Why, he asked, should a huge continent be tied to a little island thousands of miles away? Why should the colonists submit to laws that hurt their trade and industry? Why should American colonists continue swearing loyalty to a king who cared nothing for them and who had sent armies to oppress them? Everything that seemed right and reasonable demanded separation from England.

"Common Sense" became a bestseller; its simple, straightforward, and highly dramatic style made it enormously popular. Paine's writing influenced popular thought and turned independence into something demanded by enough Americans to make it politically possible.

Independence declared. Early in June of 1776 at the Second Continental Congress, one of the delegates, Richard Henry Lee of Virginia, took the floor and said that he had been directed by his colony to present the following resolution: "That these United Colonies are, and of right ought to be, free and independent States, that they are absolved from all allegiance to the British Crown, and that all political connection between them and the State of Great Britain is, and ought to be, totally dissolved."

Meanwhile, a committee was delegated to draw up a Declaration of Independence. A young man from Virginia, Thomas Jefferson, had a rare gift for expressing his thoughts in clear and inspiring words and soon had prepared a declaration for the Congress to consider.

After a few days of discussion, Congress adopted the Declaration of Independence on July 4, 1776. After long months of uncertainty, the fateful step had been taken. No longer were our forefathers fighting as British subjects for their rights in the British Empire. Now they were founders of a new nation. No longer would they refer to the "United Colonies." Now they spoke proudly of the United States of America. July 4, 1776, is one of the most significant days in American history; for it was the true beginning of the country.

The Declaration of Independence did two important things. First, it expressed a bold new idea concerning the rights of people. Before this time most men had believed that whatever rights they had were granted to them by the government under which they lived, but Jefferson believed that all men are born with certain rights that cannot be taken from them by any government. In the Declaration he expressed his belief in ringing words: "We hold these truths to be self-evident, that all men are created equal, that they are endowed by their Creator with certain unalienable rights, that among these are Life, Liberty and the pursuit of Happiness."

Jefferson went on to say that the purpose of a government is "to secure these rights," and governments must have "the consent of the governed." Whenever a government does not protect these rights or have the consent of the governed, "it is the Right of the People to alter or to abolish it." Then the people should set up a new government, in such a form as to bring about "their Safety and Happiness." Secondly, the Declaration of Independence broke all ties with England. The colonies had suffered patiently, wrote Jefferson, under the harsh laws of Great Britain. Now "it is their right, it is their duty, to throw off such Government ... WE, THEREFORE, the REPRESENTATIVES of the UNITED STATES OF AMERICA, IN GENERAL CONGRESS, Assembled ... do ... solemnly ... DECLARE, That these United Colonies are, and of Right ought to be FREE AND INDEPENDENT States." Jefferson ended the Declaration with these solemn words: "And for the support of this Declaration, with a firm reliance on the protection of Divine Providence, We Pledge to each other our Lives, our Fortunes and our sacred Honor."

The adoption of the Declaration of Independence marked a turning point in the quarrel between England and the colonies. They were forced to choose sides. For the Patriots the adoption of the Declaration was a triumph. For many of the moderates and conservatives, it was something of a personal tragedy. They now had to decide whether to support king and Parliament or to throw in their lot with the rebels.

As the news of the Declaration of Independence spread through the states, people received it with mixed feelings. Despite their happiness they wondered what would happen next. How could the United States hope to succeed against the might of England? It was one thing for Congress to declare the United States free and independent, but it would be another thing for the states to win that independence. What chance had thirteen small, poorly equipped states against the army and navy of the strongest nation in the world?

Continental army mobilized. The Patriot forces lacked training and organization. Against Britain's armies of well-trained regulars, the Patriots seem ill-matched. The men in the Continental Army had little experience in military tactics and fighting in open battle. Their training had been limited largely to frontier warfare against the Indians and the French.

Their officers had little experience compared with the British officers. The Continental army was loosely organized. Most of its men had joined, not because they had been ordered to do so, but because they wanted to join, of their own free will. Such volunteers felt free to return to their homes whenever their short terms of service were finished. As a result, the leaders of the army could hardly tell from day to day how many men were under their command. In addition, the colonies had no real navy. They did not have even one first-class man-of-war to send against the strongest navy in the world.

The Patriots also lacked equipment and money. To carry on a war, the Patriots needed equipment and supplies—muskets and cannon, bullets and powder, uniforms and food. Unfortunately, the Second Continental Congress had little money to buy these things. The Congress did not have the power to tax the people.

It could only ask the states to give money, and the sums of money received were very small. Congress tried to buy supplies with paper money, which it had printed in large quantities; but many people did not like to accept this money in payment for goods. Paper money is not worth much unless it can be exchanged for gold and silver or unless the government that issues it is strong. The Continental Congress had little gold or silver, for it was a new and weak government. As the war dragged on, Continental paper money bought less and less. "Not worth a continental" became a way of saying that something was worthless.

Complete the following statements.

2.1 To settle by agreeing that each will give up a part of what he demands is to
_____.

2.2 The Patriots captured Boston by installing _____ overlooking
the Boston Harbor.

2.3 The Second Continental Congress appointed _____ as
commander-in-chief of the colonial army.

2.4 The Congress adopted the _____ begging Parliament not to
break from the colonies until a compromise could be worked out.

2.5 Soldiers who are paid to fight for someone are called _____.

2.6 German soldiers who fought in the Revolutionary War were called _____.

2.7 The British general at the Battle of Bunker Hill was General _____.

2.8 Ethan Allen and his army captured _____
in northeastern New York.

2.9 Canada was invaded by the combined forces of _____ and
_____.

2.10 Thomas Paine wrote the pamphlet _____ which called for the
colonies to break away from _____.

2.11 The Virginian who introduced a resolution calling for freedom and independence from Great
Britain was _____.

2.12 The Virginian who was asked to draw up a declaration for independence was
_____.

2.13 The Continental Congress could not provide the army with proper equipment because it
couldn't levy _____.

2.14 The money issued by the congress wasn't worth much because they didn't have
_____ or _____ to back it up.

Place a check next to the correct answer(s).

2.15 In the Declaration of Independence, Jefferson asserts that the rights of men are:
_____ a. theirs from birth.
_____ b. given by government.
_____ c. earned.

Place a check next to the correct answer(s).

2.16 Weaknesses of the Patriot army were:
_____ a. lack of purpose
_____ b. little organization
_____ c. lack of equipment
_____ d. untrained

OPPOSITION AND AID

In spite of the difficulties of the Continental army, the Patriots fought relentlessly and kept their spirits high. The presence of the **Loyalists** helped to maintain these high spirits, for having Loyalists in their midst kept the Patriots angry. In addition, they were fighting for a common cause, which was inadvertently aided by British blunders. The aid of foreign countries and strong leaders within their own army also encouraged the Patriots to continue in their battle for independence.

Loyalist opposition. The American revolutionaries not only had to fight the forces of the king, they also had to face forces within their own villages and towns. Even after the Declaration of Independence had been signed, a large number of people, perhaps as many as a third of the colonists, remained loyal to the king. These people were known as Loyalists or Tories.

Some Loyalists merely refused to aid the Patriot cause, but others furnished food and shelter for the king's armies or actually joined the British forces. Although the Loyalists thought they were doing right, the Patriots naturally regarded them as traitors. Sometimes Loyalists were "tarred and feathered" or run out of town on a rail. Patriots attacked their homes and destroyed or seized their property. Although the tactics of the Loyalists were detrimental to the Patriots, they served as a constant reminder of what they were fighting against.

Common cause. The Patriots fought for a cause in which they believed. The Continental soldiers lacked training and supplies, but at least they were fighting in their own country. Hardy men accustomed to outdoor life, they knew how to use firearms and how to make the most of their scanty supplies. The officers and men who had fought against the French and the Indians had learned the value of alertness and self-reliance. They were fighting for a noble cause—freedom and the safety of their homes and families. The British armies, on the other hand, were filled with soldiers who had been forced into service. Far from their homelands across the ocean, the British and Hessian soldiers naturally did not fight with the same spirit as the Americans.

British blunders. In addition, the Patriots profited from mistakes which the British generals made. Many of these generals had been appointed because they had wealthy and powerful friends in the home government. They looked with contempt upon the poorly trained colonial troops and doubted they would fight very hard or very long. Like the members of an overconfident athletic team, the British commanders grew careless. Instead of striking swift, hard blows at the Continental army, they pursued it in a leisurely way. The British officers made blunders and allowed almost certain victory to slip through their fingers.

Foreign aid. The Patriots were aided by liberty-loving men from Europe who hastened to this country to serve in the Continental army. Among these volunteers was the Marquis de Lafayette. With Lafayette came the Baron de Kalb, who gave his life for American independence. Other famous foreign soldiers who joined American forces were Baron von Steuben from Prussia and Pulaski and Kosciusko from Poland. Americans were grateful for the help of these freedom-loving Europeans.

Even more important was the assistance given the United States by foreign governments. At the start of the fighting, American representatives were sent to France in the hope of obtaining aid. Because France was an old enemy of Great Britain, the Continental Congress reasoned that the French government might seize the chance to strike at the British by aiding America. Benjamin Franklin, America's wise and able statesman, worked long and hard to gain the help of France. When it appeared that the Americans had some chance of defeating the British, the French king agreed to help the Patriots. A treaty was signed by which France and the United States became military allies. France was to send money, supplies, soldiers, and ships to aid the Americans.

25

When France became our **ally**, Great Britain declared war on France. Then other European nations were drawn into the struggle. France persuaded its ally, Spain, to enter the war against Great Britain. During the later years of the war, Spanish as well as French ships kept the British navy busy. Because Dutch bankers lent money to the American states, Great Britain also declared war on Holland.

George Washington's contribution. An important reason for our country's victory was the leadership of George Washington. Washington had a good deal of military experience. He had experience in government affairs as well. His bravery and calm manner inspired officers and men alike. He refused to give up in the face of shrinking armies, lack of money and supplies, and unfair criticism. Through the darkest days of the war, Washington steadily fought on, which caused many fainthearted Patriots to be encouraged by the strength of their commander.

The courage of the Continental soldiers, the leadership of Washington, and help from foreign countries—all of these factors made possible the victory of America in the Revolutionary War. However, the struggle was not easy, nor was success certain at any time. Month after month the Patriots were called upon to meet disappointment, to endure hardship, and to fight desperately. These were, as Tom Paine wrote, "the times that try men's souls." Even when the future seemed blackest, our forefathers refused to admit defeat.

IMPORTANT CAMPAIGNS

In nearly every war, the opposing sides each experience victories and defeats, times of elation, and times of dejection. Each side inevitably makes errors in judgment and suffers for them. The Revolutionary War was no exception. Both England and the colonies gained and lost in their many campaigns. The campaigns of New York, Trenton, Princeton, Burgoyne's March on Saratoga, and the defeat of Howe in Philadelphia proved fatal for the British.

Fall of New York. In July of 1776, a large British force appeared in New York. The king wanted a quick end to the war. Washington had anticipated the British arrival and moved his army south from Boston during the spring. Placing his troops on Brooklyn Heights, a series of low hills on the western end of Long Island, he worked throughout the summer to make it another Breed's Hill.

Howe had learned his lesson, however. By carefully planning his strategy, he soundly defeated Washington, who escaped across the East River. When Howe landed on Manhattan in mid-September, Washington was forced to retreat even further north.

Washington eventually crossed the Hudson River to defend a fort in New Jersey; but Howe sent his best lieutenant, Lord Cornwallis, after him. Washington, with his deteriorating army, was no match for Cornwallis. He fled for the Delaware River, grabbed the available boats, and crossed the river to the security of Pennsylvania.

Trenton and Princeton. In December of 1776, the British were ready to stop fighting for the winter. Washington was in desperate straits. His army had dwindled to no more than five thousand, and many of those men were due to go home at New Year's. Then Washington saw his chance. The British garrison at Trenton was isolated and small; a surprise attack might capture it. On Christmas night, Washington crossed the

Delaware River, hoping to catch the Hessians in the midst of holiday celebrations. The plan worked perfectly. With scarcely a shot, Washington captured the entire garrison, though a few escaped to sound the alarm.

While Cornwallis hurried down from New York, adding to his forces as he went, Washington slipped around him and attacked Princeton, capturing that garrison and burning all its supplies. For Washington, it had been a brilliant campaign. In two short weeks he had restored American morale and regained every advantage the British had won in six months. By January of 1777, the British held New York City and nothing more.

The British were determined to make 1777 the year they would end the war and destroy the new nation. They planned to invade upper New York by way of Lake Champlain and to proceed down the Hudson River to New York City. The British thought this strategy would split the colonies and shatter American morale.

Burgoyne's march. General John Burgoyne was placed in charge of the march through New York. Burgoyne had to be stopped, but the Americans had no organized force to do it. Washington had to follow Howe who was moving south toward Philadelphia, the headquarters of the American government.

Burgoyne swept down Lake Champlain and captured the American force at Fort Ticonderoga. He then started over the mountain ridge to the Hudson River. This attempt proved slow going, for the Americans had felled trees across the road every step of the way. The farther Burgoyne went into the New York woods, the more difficult it became to advance. The Green Mountain Boys closed in behind him and threatened his supply lines. When Burgoyne sent several Hessians to Vermont to get food, they were surrounded and captured. Burgoyne still pushed on in a desperate attempt to reach Albany. There he hoped to make contact with the British army in New York City.

In Albany, General Horatio Gates was frantically building an army. Washington had lent him a few regiments, but he had to rely mainly on the New England militiamen who had flooded into his headquarters after Burgoyne's Indian allies attacked a few pioneer families. Throughout the war, several tribes of Indians fought with the colonists, and some sided with the British.

Gates placed his army on Bemis Heights with the river on one side and woods on the other. Fighting began on September 19, when the colonial regiment of Virginia sharpshooters began sniping at the British troops from the woods and ended on October 7, when an American detachment led by Benedict Arnold crushed the British force. Ten days later at the nearby town of Saratoga, Burgoyne surrendered his entire army. The Battle of Saratoga was the turning point in America's fight for independence since it dashed any hopes the British had of isolating New England from the rest of the colonies.

Fall of Philadelphia. The campaign of General Howe fared somewhat better. He sailed from New York in July of 1777, leaving Sir Henry Clinton in command of the city, with orders to aid Burgoyne.

Suspecting that Howe was bound for Philadelphia, Washington moved south and met Howe in September of 1777 at Brandywine Creek, near the Pennsylvania-Delaware border. Despite Washington's efforts to hold the British back, Howe slipped past the American forces and took Philadelphia. Washington retired to Valley Forge and went into winter quarters.

When Benjamin Franklin, serving as American envoy to France, was told that Howe had taken the American capital, he replied: "I beg your pardon, sir. Philadelphia has taken Howe."

The city was a comfortable place to spend a winter, but it had no other military advantages. Howe controlled the city, and that was all. In European warfare the capture of a capital city was enough to end a war. This did not occur in America. The Continental Congress, having fled Philadelphia, simply continued congressional sessions in York, Pennsylvania.

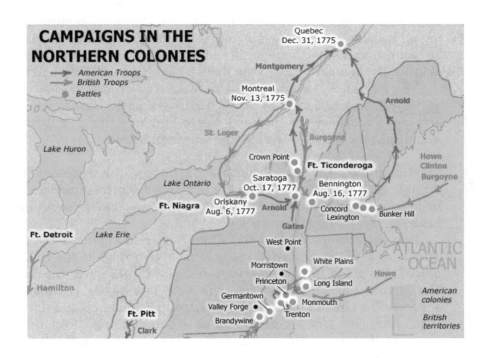

CAMPAIGNS IN THE NORTHERN COLONIES

American Troops
British Troops
● Battles

Quebec
Dec. 31, 1775

Montgomery

Montreal
Nov. 13, 1775

Arnold

St. Leger

Burgoyne

Lake Huron

Crown Point

Ft. Ticonderoga

Howe
Clinton
Burgoyne

Lake Ontario

Saratoga
Oct. 17, 1777

Bennington
Aug. 16, 1777

Ft. Niagra

Oriskany
Aug. 6, 1777

Arnold

Concord
Lexington

Bunker Hill

Ft. Detroit

Lake Erie

Gates

West Point

ATLANTIC
OCEAN

Morristown

White Plains

Howe

Hamilton

Princeton

Long Island

American
colonies

Ft. Pitt

Germantown
Valley Forge ●

Monmouth

Trenton

British
territories

Brandywine

Clark

WINTER AT VALLEY FORGE

While the British enjoyed Philadelphia's social life, Washington and his ill-equipped, poorly clothed, and untrained army froze at Valley Forge. Washington reported at one point that almost 3,000 men were unfit for duty because they were barefoot and poorly clothed. With men hungry, sick, and freezing, morale and discipline were low for the Patriot army, but things were soon to take a turn for the better.

During the winter a German officer appeared in camp. He identified himself as Baron von Steuben, general in the army of the European king Frederick the Great. Although he had exaggerated his rank (he was really only a captain) and his title (he had none), von Steuben made a good impression. Some of the foreign arrivals had embarrassed Washington by demanding instant command, but von Steuben merely offered to be helpful. Washington made him Inspector General and asked him to train his soldiers.

The task was not easy, since Americans did not take kindly to military discipline, but von Steuben managed to set up a system that worked. He taught the soldiers how to drill with muskets, how to march in step, and how to switch ranks from marching column to battle formation. He taught them how to fight in a professional manner.

HISTORY & GEOGRAPHY

1 1 0 2

LIFEPAC TEST

70 / 87

Name _____

Date _____

Score _____

HISTORY & GEOGRAPHY 1102: LIFEPAC TEST

Answer *true* **or** *false* (each answer, 1 point).

1. _____ England began to tax the colonies heavily to help pay for the French and Indian War.
2. _____ The American navy, under the command of John Paul Jones, was no match for the British naval forces.
3. _____ During the post-Revolutionary period, most of the states passed laws forbidding the further importation of slaves.
4. _____ Shays' Rebellion was an armed uprising of western farmers who were enraged over economic discontent and heavy taxation.
5. _____ The Constitution was merely a revision of the Articles of Confederation.
6. _____ The Federalist papers of 1788 were a series of newspaper articles written in support of the Constitution by Hamilton, Madison, and Jay.
7. _____ After crossing the Delaware on Christmas night, 1776, Washington and his troops were victorious in the Battles of Trenton and Princeton.

Match these items (each answer, 2 points).

8. _____ Declaratory Law   a. established Fort Necessity
9. _____ Cornwallis   b. surrendered at Yorktown
10. _____ Federalists   c. allowed British to search colonists' homes
11. _____ Virginia Resolves   d. result of Stamp Act
12. _____ First Navigation Act   e. opposed Constitution
13. _____ Washington   f. settlers not permitted to move west
14. _____ Proclamation Act of 1763   g. ships had to be English
15. _____ Writs of assistance   h. British commander at Vincennes
16. _____ Antifederalist   i. Parliament allowed to pass any laws
17. _____ Colonel Hamilton   j. favored Constitution

Place a check beside the correct answers (each lettered blank, 1 point).

18. Two strengths the Continental army possessed were
    a. _____ fighting for a common cause.
    b. _____ intense training.
    c. _____ the quality and quantity of equipment.
    d. _____ making use of British mistakes.
    e. _____ organization

19. Three weaknesses of the Continental army were
    a. _____ lack of purpose.
    b. _____ little organization.
    c. _____ lack of equipment.
    d. _____ untrained.

Write the letter of the correct answer on the blank (each answer, 2 points).

20. Thomas Paine wrote _____ .
    a. *The Federalist Papers*
    b. the Constitution
    c. *Common Sense*

21. Congress adopted the _____
    a. Olive Branch Petition begging Parliament not to break from the colonies until a compromise could be worked out.
    b. Virginia Plan begging Parliament not to break from the colonies until a compromise could be worked out.
    c. Treaty of Paris begging Parliament not to break from the colonies until a compromise could be worked out.

22. The Declaration of Independence was drawn up by _____ .
    a. Benjamin Franklin
    b. Thomas Jefferson
    c. James Madison

23. Another name for a Loyalist was _____ .
    a. Tory
    b. Patriot
    c. Hessian

24. In 1776 Howe defeated _____ .
    a. General Burgoyne in New York
    b. General Gates in New York
    c. George Washington in New York

25. The hero at Saratoga was _____ .
    a. Horatio Gates
    b. George Rogers Clark
    c. Nathaniel Greene

26. The Intolerable Acts were passed to _____ .
    a. prevent a war
    b. punish Boston
    c. increase trade

27. Congress didn't provide the army with enough equipment because _____ .
    a. they didn't want a war
    b. they wanted foreign countries to give aid
    c. they didn't have enough money

28. Which man did General Washington make the Chief Inspector of the colonial troops? _____
    a. Lafayette
    b. Baron von Steuben
    c. Greene

29. The last state to ratify the Constitution was _____ .
    a. Rhode Island
    b. Georgia
    c. Connecticut
30. Passage of the Townshend Acts caused the colonists to _____ .
    a. revolt
    b. urge Congress to veto the Act
    c. boycott English goods
    d. go on a hunger strike
31. The Committees of Correspondence were organized by _____ .
    a. Samuel Adams
    b. James Otis
    c. Patrick Henry
    d. Paul Revere

Complete the following statements (each answer, 3 points).

32. The "Great Compromise" of the Constitution suggested a two-part legislature consisting of a
    _____ and a _____ .
33. The Constitution provides for a three-branch system consisting of the _____ ,
    _____ , and _____ branches, which makes possible the system
    of " _____ and _____ ."
34. The Northwest Ordinance of 1787 provided _____ for the Northwest.
35. One weakness of the British army was fighting on _____ .

NOTES

Match the words with their correct definitions.

2.17 _____ ally

2.18 _____ treaty

2.19 _____ Loyalist

a. colonist who opposed independence for the American colonies at the time of the American Revolutionary War

b. an agreement, especially one between nations, signed and approved by each nation

c. a person, group or nation united with another for some special purpose

Complete the following statements.

2.20 Five important sites or battles in the Revolutionary War were

a. _____ , b. _____ ,

c. _____ , d. _____ ,

and e. _____ .

2.21 Loyalists supported the _____ .

2.22 "Tory" is another name for _____ .

2.23 Cornwallis was a _____ commander.

2.24 In July, 1776, Howe defeated _____ in New York.

2.25 Washington defeated Cornwallis at _____ .

2.26 Three factors which made possible the victory of America in the Revolutionary War were

a. _____

b. _____

c. _____

2.27 Washington made von Steuben the _____ .

True/False.

2.28 _____ The British thought that by invading New York at Lake Champlain and proceeding down the Hudson River to New York City, they would divide the colonies and shatter their morale.

2.29 _____ Valley Forge was a high point in the American Revolution.

Place a check beside the correct answers.

2.30 Von Steuben aided the Patriots by teaching the soldiers which four of the following things?

_____ a. drill with muskets

_____ b. dress in uniform properly

_____ c. clean their muskets

_____ d. march in step.

_____ e. switch ranks

_____ f. pull rank

_____ g. fight professionally

WAR IN THE SOUTH AND WEST

While Washington and his troops froze in Valley Forge, General Howe enjoyed the comforts of Philadelphia. However, taking the city gave no military advantage to the British, and General Howe was soon to be replaced.

General Howe turned over his command to Sir Henry Clinton in 1778. Clinton, who had never approved of the Philadelphia venture, resolved to leave the city and to return the army to New York.

Battle of Monmouth. Washington followed the strung-out British forces and pounced on them at Monmouth court house in New Jersey. In a day-long battle on an extremely hot day in June, the two armies fought to a draw. The next morning the British resumed their march to New York, leaving Washington with the field of battle and a technical victory.

War continues. After this battle the war in the north died down and the scene of action shifted to the South. Except for an unsuccessful British attack on Charleston in South Carolina, at the beginning of the war, the South had so far escaped the fighting. This fact in itself was strange, for the southern colonies were the most valuable of all. The British may have avoided war with the South because the South grew tobacco, rice, indigo, and other staples that Britain could not produce. The surplus from these crops brought a handsome profit in England and in Europe. The southern colonies imported most of their manufactured foods and depended on Britain for banking services.

The Loyalists had, until this time, maintained their allegiance to the king of England. At the prospect of losing their homes and property to invading British forces, they became convinced that they really were in favor of independence after all. The British hopes that loyal colonists would aid their cause in the South were largely unrealized.

In December of 1778 a British army under the command of Lord Cornwallis landed at Savannah and overtook Georgia. Congress hastily organized a southern army and placed Benjamin Lincoln in command. Lincoln and the British maneuvered through the tidal swamps of South Carolina for a year, until General Clinton bottled up Lincoln in Charleston and forced his surrender in May of 1780. The loss of Lincoln's army was the biggest American defeat of the war. Confident that South Carolina was under control, Clinton left for New York.

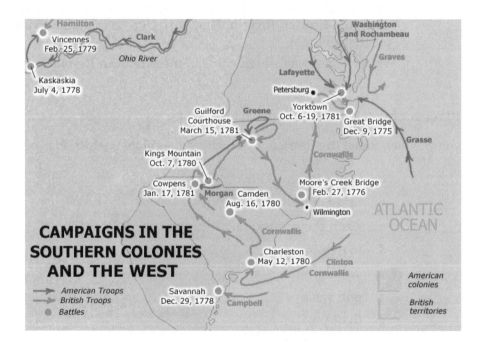

CAMPAIGNS IN THE SOUTHERN COLONIES AND THE WEST

→ American Troops
→ British Troops
● Battles

30

Defeat of Gates. Congress designated the hero of Saratoga, Horatio Gates, as the new commander in the South. Gates encountered Cornwallis at Camden in South Carolina. At the sight of British bayonets, Gates' militia panicked and fled, sweeping their commander along with them. Congress fired Gates and asked Washington to name a new commander in the South. Washington selected Nathaniel Greene, who had been a Rhode Island bookseller before the war.

Greene's command. By the time Greene arrived in the South, the situation had changed considerably. Two victories had eliminated Cornwallis' western flank, which enabled Greene to concentrate on the main army of the British.

Greene shrewdly let Cornwallis roam the woods of North Carolina without risking his own force in battle. Cornwallis soon made the same discovery Burgoyne had. He had marched "triumphantly" for hundreds of miles and found himself in possession of nothing but the soil under his feet. In March of 1781, Greene at last gave battle at Guilford, North Carolina, and the two armies fought to a draw. Frantic for a victory, Cornwallis pursued him, but Greene slipped nimbly into Virginia.

WAR IN THE WEST

On the frontier, the fighting was carried on mostly by the Indians. The British told the Indians that if the colonists won the Indians would be pushed out of their hunting grounds, and colonists would build their farms there. The English are reported to have given gifts to the Indian braves who brought human scalps to them. A bold young frontiersman named George Rogers Clark decided to put an end to the Indian attacks in the West. He led a force of men down the Ohio River, surprising and capturing the British frontier forts in the present-day states of Illinois and Indiana.

He left a small force at Vincennes in what is now Indiana. Colonel Hamilton, the British commander, recaptured the fort. He anticipated that the Americans would try to take the fort again, but he believed that they would wait until spring. However, Clark led a small group of men through

George Rogers Clark

ice and snow to recapture the fort. Clark's victories gave the Americans a hold on the vast area of land between the Great Lakes, the Ohio River, and the Mississippi River. After Clark's campaign, the Indians were less of a menace on the frontier.

AMERICAN NAVY

From the harbors of New England, fishing vessels, and merchant ships that had been equipped with guns and crews sailed forth to seize enemy shipping. These **privateers**, as they were called, captured many a British merchant vessel and brought it to port. The cargo of the captured ship was then sold and the money divided among the crew of the privateer. Later in the war, as British man-of-wars kept a close watch along the coast for privateers, fewer American ships cared to venture out.

When they were colonists of Britain, the Americans had no navy. They had always depended on the British fleet for protection. Now this fleet was fighting against them, not for them. Early in the war Congress had begun to build a navy. John Paul Jones, a Scottish seaman who had settled in Virginia, advised Congress to build small, speedy ships. During the whole of the Revolutionary War, however, the United States Navy had only about forty ships. Before the end of the war, all but six of these were either captured or sunk by their crews to prevent the enemy from taking them.

Although small, the American navy gave a good account of itself. The most famous sea battle of the Revolution took place between a British man-of-war and a ship built in France and commanded by John Paul Jones. Jones had been cruising along the British coast with his vessel, the *Bonhomme Richard*, and three other ships. Coming upon a fleet of merchant ships guarded by two British warships, he attacked the larger enemy warship, called the *Serapis*.

During the bloody three-hour battle, the *Bonhomme Richard* suffered great damage and was leaking badly. Jones ran his ship so close to the *Serapis* that their cannons almost touched. The British commander called out, "Have you lowered your flag?" In words that have become famous, Jones replied, "I have not yet begun to fight," and went on shooting. Soon the decks of the *Bonhomme Richard* were littered with dead and wounded men, but the *Serapis* was also badly damaged. When its mainmast fell, the British commander surrendered to Jones.

John Paul Jones had shown that Americans could fight on sea as well as on land. Although Jones spent most of his later life in Europe, his body was brought back to the United States after his death. He now lies in an honored grave at the Naval Academy in Annapolis.

HEROES AND TRAITORS

In any war there are heroes and traitors, people who add tremendously to the cause and those who seek to destroy it. The two men best known for such acts were Nathan Hale and Benedict Arnold.

Nathan Hale. Soon after the British had taken control of New York City, Washington was interested in finding out the plans of the British. He called for volunteers to go into New York City to spy. One of the volunteers was twenty-one-year-old Captain Nathan Hale. In disguise, Hale made his way into New York City, but was captured by the British and hanged as a spy. As Nathan Hale faced death his last words were: "I only regret that I have but one life to lose for my country."

Benedict Arnold. An event of another sort occurred in 1780. Among the Patriot leaders who fought brilliantly early in the war was Benedict Arnold. He had attacked Quebec at the start of the war and had taken part in the Battle of Saratoga, which led to Burgoyne's surrender. Arnold was an ambitious man who felt that he deserved more credit than he had received for his services to the Patriot cause. Instead, he was criticized and court-martialed for misusing his powers as military governor of Philadelphia. Moreover, Arnold had fallen deeply into debt. His need for money and his wounded pride tempted him to enter the pay of the British. He not only furnished the British with military secrets but influenced Washington to place him in command of the fort at West Point, New York. Arnold planned to turn over the fort to the British.

The plot to surrender West Point was discovered in 1780 by the capture of Major Andre, the English officer with whom Arnold was dealing. Andre was executed as a spy, but Arnold managed to reach the British lines in safety. During the remainder of the war he fought under the British flag. Years later he died in England, an unhappy man. His name came to mean traitor in his native land, and he was looked upon with contempt, even in England.

BATTLE OF YORKTOWN

Cornwallis was convinced that to hold the Carolinas he would have to take Virginia. He decided to act. In April of 1781, he started north, expecting Greene to follow. Instead, Greene slipped around the British forces and headed for South Carolina. While Cornwallis rampaged across Virginia, Greene captured, one by one, the British outposts holding South Carolina. Unfortunately, Greene's action left Virginia at the mercy of Cornwallis.

Washington sent Lafayette south to keep an eye on Cornwallis, giving him command of a few regiments of Virginian and Maryland Continentals. After von Steuben and another officer, Anthony Wayne, joined forces with Lafayette, Cornwallis retired to Yorktown near Chesapeake Bay to await relief forces from New York. Lafayette set up camp at Williamsburg and sent a letter to General Washington.

If Washington could bring the main army south before the relief ships arrived, wrote Lafayette, Cornwallis might be trapped. Fortunately, Lafayette's letter arrived at Washington's New York headquarters along with word from French Admiral De Grasse that the French fleet would be in American waters that summer.

Washington then ordered De Grasse to Chesapeake Bay to blockade Cornwallis and quickly headed south. De Grasse ferried him down Chesapeake Bay, and the combined French-American force joined Lafayette outside Yorktown. When the British relief force arrived, the two fleets fought a battle that neither side won, although it was enough to send the British ships back to New York for repairs. Cornwallis was trapped!

On October 19, 1781, Cornwallis surrendered his army. The fighting was over, for Greene was in possession of South Carolina, and the British were back where they started. They held New York and Charleston, and that was all. They evacuated Charleston at the end of the year and New York in December of 1782, after the first articles of peace were signed.

Answer *true* **or** *false*.

2.31 _____ The British maintained their occupation of Philadelphia since it gave them such a tremendous military advantage.

2.32 _____ The Patriots achieved a clear victory at the Battle of Monmouth by soundly defeating the British forces.

2.33 _____ Congress designated the hero of Saratoga, General Horatio Gates, as the new commander in the South.

2.34 _____ The colonial forces under Gates' command fought bravely against the British at Camden, South Carolina.

2.35 _____ Clark was not able to maintain his hold on the fort in Vincennes, and it was retaken by Colonel Hamilton and his troops.

2.36 _____ Clark surprised Colonel Hamilton by attacking Vincennes in the winter and recapturing the fort.

Complete the following statements.

2.37 The new commander who replaced Gates in the South was _____ .

2.38 George Rogers Clark captured the British frontier forts in the present states of

_____ and _____ .

2.39 Clark's victories gave the Americans a hold on the land between the

_____ , the _____ and the

_____ .

2.40 During the Revolutionary War, only about _____ ships were in the United States Navy.

2.41 John Paul Jones replied to the captain of the *Serapis*, "I have not _____

_____ ."

2.42 An armed ship privately owned but armed for war is a _____ .

2.43 The French ship in the most famous sea fight of the Revolutionary War was commanded by

_____ .

2.44 Benedict Arnold planned to turn American fort of _____ over to Major Andre.

2.45 Benedict Arnold had a leading part in the Battle of _____ before he changed sides.

2.46 Nathan Hale: "I only regret _____ ."

2.47 Cornwallis was convinced that in order to hold the Carolinas he would have to take

_____ .

Match these men with the best possible definition.

2.48 _____ George Rogers Clark   a. gave his life for his country

2.49 _____ Nathan Hale   b. betrayed his country

2.50 _____ Benedict Arnold   c. captured the west from the British

2.51 _____ John Paul Jones   d. British commander at Vincennes

2.52 _____ Colonel Hamilton   e. American navy officer

Write the letter of the correct answer on the line.

2.53 Cornwallis was defeated at Yorktown because _____

a. his troops were wounded and sick.

b. French and American ships kept relief forces from arriving.

c. Greene had followed him from North Carolina.

d. his position near Chesapeake Bay was hard to defend.

Adult Check _____

    Initial   Date

Review the material in this section in preparation for the Self Test. The Self Test will check your mastery of this section and the previous section.

SELF TEST 2

Answer *true* **or** *false* (each answer, 1 point).

2.01 _____ If the British had accepted the Olive Branch Petition, the Revolutionary War might have been averted.

2.02 _____ Although the colonial army lacked equipment and money at the beginning of the war, Congress could levy taxes which would alleviate the problem.

2.03 _____ The British general at the Battle of Bunker Hill was Horatio Gates.

2.04 _____ Patriots not only backed England's actions, they also aided the British army by giving them food and money.

2.05 _____ The victory at Trenton was important because it caused France to sign a treaty with America that would provide the aid America so desperately needed.

2.06 _____ The British attempt to cut New England off from the rest of the colonies failed when Burgoyne surrendered his army at Saratoga.

2.07 _____ Lord Grenville's program included the Virginia Resolves.

2.08 _____ The first direct tax levied by England on the colonists was the Stamp Tax.

2.09 _____ The Intolerable Acts were aimed at punishing Boston for its infamous Tea Party.

Match each of these items with the best possible description (each answer, 2 points).

2.010 _____ Battle of Bunker Hill   a. Declaration of Independence

2.011 _____ Ethan Allan   b. Breeds Hill's

2.012 _____ Hessians   c. commander-in-chief of the Continental army

2.013 _____ Thomas Paine   d. American traitor

2.014 _____ Thomas Jefferson   e. secured the western lands

2.015 _____ George Washington   f. mercenaries from Germany

2.016 _____ Nathan Hale   g. "I have not yet begun to fight."

2.017 _____ Benedict Arnold   h. *Common Sense*

2.018 _____ John Paul Jones   i. seized Fort Ticonderoga

2.019 _____ George Rogers Clark   j. "I only regret that I have but one life to lose for my country."

Write the letter of the correct answer on the line (each answer, 2 points).

2.020 The Second Continental Congress _____
   a. made provisions for a Continental army with George Washington as commander in-chief.
   b. adopted a "Declaration of Causes of Necessity of Taking up Arms."
   c. endorsed the Olive Branch Petition.
   d. all of the above.

2.021 The Proclamation Act of 1763 _____
   a. allowed Parliament to pass all laws.
   b. was the final act that angered the colonies to such an extent that they went to war.
   c. closed the lands west of the Allegheny Mountains to settlers.
   d. led to the formation of the Sons of Liberty.

Place a check beside the correct answers (each lettered blank, 1 points).

2.022   The Declaration of Independence

_____   a. was an opportunity for education.

_____   b. did not completely sever ties with England.

_____   c. expressed the idea that all men are created equal and are born with certain rights that no government can take from them.

_____   d. was adopted on July 4, 1776.

2.023   America's victory in the Revolutionary War was made more probable

_____   a. because George Washington was an excellent leader.

_____   b. through money, supplies, soldiers, and ships that were presented through foreign aid from France.

_____   c. because of serious blunders on the part of the British commanders.

_____   d. because the colonists were courageous in fighting for a cause in which they believed.

_____   e. because England hired the Hessian mercenaries.

2.024   The Committees of Correspondence

_____   a. were formed to encourage communication among the colonies.

_____   b. wrote the Declaration of Rights and Grievances.

_____   c. were led by John Adams.

_____   d. used fast riders to send the news.

_____   e. succeeded because England hired the Hessian mercenaries.

_____   f. wrote essays about the citizen's freedom.

_____   g. enforced voting rights.

2.025   What were two disadvantages the colonies faced in starting a war with England?

_____   a. lack of money and equipment

_____   b. needed a cause

_____   c. lack of strong leaders

_____   d. lack of organization

2.026   What were two advantages England had in fighting a war in America?

_____   a. well-trained soldiers

_____   b. money and equipment

_____   c. British commanders were decisive striking swift hard blows to the patriots.

_____   d. familiarity with the land

Complete the following statements (each answer, 2 points).

2.027 The British commander who surrendered at Yorktown was _____.

2.028 The colonist who convinced the French to aid the colonies was _____.

2.029 The _____ stated that certain rights were not given by the government but that men were born with them.

2.030 "If this be treason, make the most of it," was said by _____.

Match each word with its correct definition (each answer, 2 points).

2.031 _____ boycott

a. a soldier hired for pay by a foreign state

2.032 _____ ally

b. to settle (a quarrel or difference of opinion) by agreeing that each will give up a part of what he demands

2.033 _____ Loyalist

c. an agreement, especially one between nations, signed and approved by each nation

2.034 _____ treaty

d. a person, group, or nation united with another for some special purpose

2.035 _____ compromise

e. an American colonist who opposed independence for the American colonies

2.036 _____ mercenary

f. to join together against and have nothing to do with

62/77

Score
Adult Check

_____
_____
Initial   Date

37

III. BIRTH OF A NATION

Even before the struggle for American independence had been successfully concluded, members of the Second Continental Congress had taken steps to establish a central government for the thirteen states. The government established by the Articles of Confederation understandably bore little resemblance to the English model. The Articles provided for no chief executive who might act like a king and no central courts that might overrule the decisions of state courts. Congress was even denied the right to levy or collect taxes, lest it follow Parliament's practice of taxing unfairly.

By the mid-1780s, it was clear that the Articles of Confederation left too much power in the hands of the states. Nevertheless, efforts to amend the Articles ended in failure. Finally, a convention was called to meet in Philadelphia to devise a new government. The product of its deliberations was the Constitution. The new plan of government enlarged legislative powers of the government and provided for a chief executive and a system of national courts. But the most important achievement of the Constitutional Convention was the distribution of power between the states and the federal government. The founding fathers sought to establish an effective central government and at the same time to preserve the rights of the states.

To George Washington fell the task of translating the Constitution into a functioning government. His political associates, the Federalists, thought that the federal government should be stronger than the states. Soon, however, an opposition group was formed that wanted to limit the powers of the federal government. After 1800 the Democratic-Republicans controlled both Congress and the Presidency. Delegates to the Constitutional Convention had feared that political parties would create conflict within the nation, but their appearance at an early date was a fortunate development, for they provided various groups with an opportunity to state their opinions and grievances.

SECTION OBJECTIVES

Review these objectives. When you have completed this section, you should be able to:

9. Name the provisions of the Treaty of Paris of 1783.
10. State the strengths and weaknesses of the Articles of Confederation.
11. Describe the conflicting proposals of the Constitutional Convention.
12. Name the three branches of government and describe the system of checks and balances.
13. Explain the land ordinances of 1785 and 1787.
14. Describe the objections to and provisions of the Constitution.

VOCABULARY

Study these words to enhance your learning success in this section.

democracy	A government run by the people who live under it; people rule either directly through meetings that all may attend, or indirectly through the election of representatives
emancipation	The act or process of setting free from slavery of any kind; release
Antifederalist	A member of the political party that opposed the adoption of the Constitution of the United States before 1789
Federalist	A member of the political party in the United States that favored the adoption of the Constitution and later, the establishment of a strong central government; the party existed from about 1791 to 1816
ratification	Confirmation; approval

COLONIAL PEACE

Congress had disbanded the Continental army on November 3, 1782; and on December 4, George Washington said farewell to his officers at Fraunces Tavern in New York. He then traveled to Annapolis, Maryland, where Congress was in session and on December 23 formally resigned his commission. For eight and one-half years he had served as general, through defeat and disaster, through unrelenting weather and through congressional incapacity; and he had kept firmly and unwaveringly to a difficult task.

The result was not only victory for his forces, but the steady admiration of Americans for Washington through all their history. In addition, Washington's action in retiring rather than trying to use his popularity to gain political power was much admired both at home and abroad.

Treaty of Paris. Although the actual fighting in America was over in 1781, the war was not officially over until the signing of the Treaty of Paris of 1783. By this treaty Great Britain recognized the United States as an independent nation. The new territory of the nation was to stretch from Canada to Florida and from the Atlantic Ocean to the Mississippi River. The river itself, however, was to be open to the trade of both Great Britain and the United States.

American fishermen were to be permitted to fish off Newfoundland and the mouth of the St. Lawrence River. In a separate treaty, Great Britain returned Florida to Spain. King George III said sourly that considering the "knavery" of the Americans perhaps it might

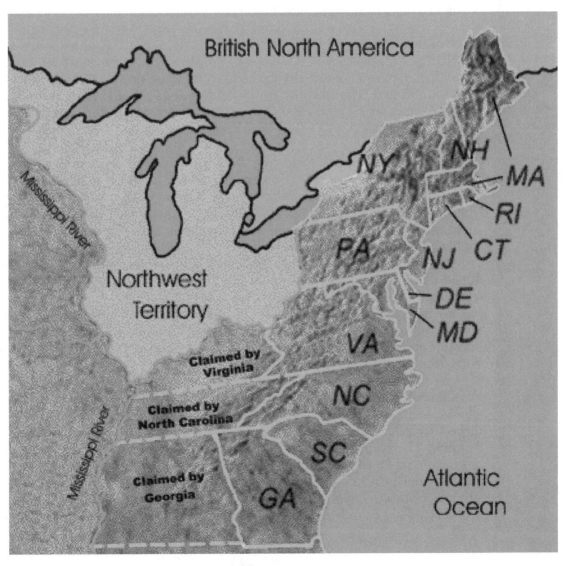

"not in the end be an evil" that they had left the British Empire. As for the Americans, the opinions of George III were no longer important to them. They had won their freedom and founded a new nation.

The scars of war were comparatively light. The cities had been left untouched and, except for the Tory and Indian raids, no real atrocities existed. American casualties may have been nineteen thousand wounded with about four thousand listed as killed in action. The British casualties are not known but are estimated to have been at least twice as high as the American figures.

The greatest tragedy befell the Loyalists, who had fought for what they considered their country and king. Had the American rebellion been crushed, they would have been heroes; as it was, they were traitors. The best thing they could do was to leave a country that was now actively hostile toward them. On April 26, 1783, seven thousand Loyalists left New York City as refugees. Some went to Great Britain and some to Canada. Many others also fled or were driven out. Estimates place the total number of Loyalist refugees at one hundred thousand. Many thousands of others remained, suffering various degrees of ill treatment until the passions of the war subsided.

The British left also. Through November, the British in New York were pulling back and preparing to embark. By November 25, 1783, the British had left New York City, and on December 4 they left Staten Island.

The Revolution did more than sever American ties with Great Britain, it brought about changes in the new nation itself. New state governments were established. The state legislatures introduced social and economic changes that affected the American people, who by 1790 numbered about four million. The chief problem in the years following the Treaty of Paris in 1783 was the creation of a central government.

Colonial changes. A political **democracy** needs a strong social foundation if it is to survive. A democracy will always be shaky if great gaps exist between rich and poor, if conflicts develop between loyalties to church and nation, or if the people are illiterate and uninformed. The Revolution brought changes in all these areas, and these social changes were as important to the future of American democracy as the changes in political structure.

State governments. Since the Declaration of Independence had made the colonies free and independent states, it became necessary for them to develop state governments. The Americans wanted written documents similar to the charters that they already had. Rhode Island and Connecticut were able to use their charters with only a few minor revisions. The other colonies wrote new constitutions. Most of them included a list of personal rights guaranteed to each citizen.

The new state governments had many features in common. Each constitution gave broad powers to the legislature and most states had legislatures with two houses. Each state legislature kept tight control over taxation. Each constitution provided for a government whose powers were strictly limited and each listed the qualifications for holding office and for voting. To run for office a man had to pay a certain amount of taxes or own a certain amount of property. Voting requirements were similar. Only Vermont had suffrage for all men over twenty-one years of age.

Church and state. Many of the state constitutions provided for the separation of church and state affairs, which meant that the government could not support an established church. Thomas Jefferson and James Madison led the fight for separation in Virginia. The adoption of their bill in 1786 set an important precedent, for most earlier governments combined church and state. By the end of the Revolutionary War, most states had adopted the principle of separation of church and state. Only in New England did the church maintain an established position, and it was not until the 1830s that the Congregational churches of New England became completely separate from the state.

Land ownership. Americans were quick to grasp the economic opportunity that opened following the Revolution. Land became more plentiful. Thousands pushed into the lands beyond the Appalachian Mountains that had been closed by the Proclamation Line of 1763. In addition, the land belonging to English proprietors or to the king, as well as the land seized from the Loyalists, was divided into small parcels and sold at reasonable prices. Small farmers now had an opportunity to buy land in already settled areas of the country.

Slavery. A number of Americans began to speak out against slavery. The original draft of the Declaration of Independence condemned slave trade, but this section was deleted from the final draft. By 1786 all states except Georgia had banned the importing of slaves. Ironically, the last state to ban importing slaves was the first one to have originally banned slavery. Rhode Island freed its slaves before the Revolutionary War while Pennsylvania and Massachusetts abolished slavery during the war. Other northern states gradually established **emancipation** for slaves.

The South found the problem more difficult because of the large number of slaves. Prominent southerners like Patrick Henry, Thomas Jefferson, and George Washington felt that slavery was not consistent with the belief in human rights. George Washington freed his slaves in his will. Other planters took similar action, but none of the southern states proposed practical ways of ending slavery.

Education. Americans were aware of the need for a good education. Some proposed the establishment of public schools, but these schools were not to be founded for some years yet. Nevertheless, Massachusetts maintained its constitutional law requiring local support for public schools. In the meantime, private academies educated the sons of well-to-do families. Education eventually became available for most American children. Colleges were also established in America, and the number of them increased, providing many with the opportunity for a higher education.

Fill in the blanks.

3.1   A _____ is a government run by the people who live under it.

3.2   The act or process of setting free from slavery of any kind is called _____ .

3.3   In a separate treaty, Great Britain returned Florida to _____ .

3.4   The number of Loyalists who left the United States is estimated at _____ .

3.5   American casualties may have been _____ wounded and _____ killed.

3.6   The last British troops left Staten Island on _____ .

3.7   General George Washington gave his farewell address to his troops at _____ in New York.

3.8   The first state to have suffrage for all men over twenty-one years of age was _____ .

3.9   " _____ of church and _____ " is what happens when the government cannot support an established church.

3.10   The first state to free slaves was _____ .

3.11   Slavery was abolished in _____ and _____ during the Revolutionary War.

3.12   The slave owner who freed his slaves in his will was _____ .

3.13   The constitution of Massachusetts required local support of _____ schools.

ARTICLES OF CONFEDERATION

The Second Continental Congress served as a temporary government for the states immediately after the Revolutionary War began. The delegates began almost immediately to plan for a permanent government. A committee was appointed in 1776 to draw up a constitution for the United States. This plan was submitted to the states for acceptance in 1777. However, not until 1781 did all of the states ratify the new government and its constitution, known as the *Articles of Confederation*.

(10)

A R T I C L E S

OF

CONFEDERATION and PERPETUAL UNION

BETWEEN THE STATES OF

NEW-HAMPSHIRE, MASSACHUSETTS-BAY, RHODE-ISLAND and PROVIDENCE PLANTATIONS, CONNECTICUT, NEW-YORK, NEW-JERSEY, PENNSYLVANIA, DELAWARE, MARYLAND, VIRGINIA, NORTH-CAROLINA, SOUTH-CAROLINA, and GEORGIA.

ARTICLE I.

THE ftile of this confederacy fhall be, "UNITED STATES OF AMERICA."

ARTICLE II.

Each State retains its fovereignty, freedom, and independence, and every power, jurifdiction, and right, which is not by this confederation exprefsly delegated to the United States in Congrefs affembled.

ARTICLE III.

The faid States hereby feverally enter into a firm league of friendfhip with each other, for their common defence, the fecurity of their liberties, and

ARTICLES OF CONFEDERATION.

and their mutual and general welfare, binding themfelves to affift each other againft all force offered to, or attacks made upon them, or any of them, on account of religion, fovereignty, trade, or any other pretence whatever.

ARTICLE IV.

The better to fecure and perpetuate mutual friendfhip and intercourfe among the people of the different States in this union, the free inhabitants of each of thefe States, paupers, vagabonds, and fugitives from juftice excepted, fhall be entitled to all privileges and immunities of free citizens in the feveral States; and the people of each State fhall have free ingrefs and regrefs to and from any other State, and fhall enjoy therein all the privileges of trade and commerce, fubject to the fame duties, impofitions, and reftrictions, as the inhabitants thereof refpectively, provided that fuch reftrictions fhall not extend fo far as to prevent the removal of property imported into any State to any other State of which the owner is an inhabitant; provided alfo that no impofition, duties, or reftriction, fhall be laid by any State on the property of the United States, or either of them.

If

The delay concerned the claims of a number of states to the land west of the Allegheny Mountains. Seven states claimed that their charters had given them the rights to great stretches of land beyond these mountains and extending to the Mississippi River. The states without these claims wanted the other states to surrender their claims to the national government. Maryland refused to accept the new constitution until this matter had been settled by the government. Finally, all the states gave up their claims and on March 21, 1781, a new government began operating under the Articles of Confederation, replacing the Second Continental Congress.

Weakness of the Articles. Under the Articles of Confederation, the government consisted of a loose confederation of thirteen states. During this critical period the government was extremely weak and inefficient because it lacked powers necessary for a strong national government.

The Articles of Confederation were flawed by many weaknesses and inadequacies. The equal voting power in Congress led to jealousies and fights between large states (like Virginia with almost 450,000 people) and small states (like Rhode Island with 65,000 people). The big states wanted more voting power than the small states because they were larger, richer, and more heavily populated.

Another problem was that, although it could levy taxes, Congress was not given the power to collect them. The result was that it never had enough money to run an efficient government. Congress also lacked the power to control trade and commerce between the states or between the United States and other countries. No system of national courts was provided in which to try the violators of the national laws. All cases were tried in state courts, where the judges tended to be lenient toward such violators.

The individual states enforced the laws of the Confederation Congress; and the states were not in favor of giving too much power to the national government and especially to any form of executive, like a president. To pass laws, the vote of nine of the thirteen states was necessary. This majority was not easy to achieve, particularly since a number of states would not even send representatives to Congress.

Problems under the Articles of Confederation

A unanimous vote of all the thirteen states was necessary to amend the Articles of Confederation. This vote was almost an impossibility because at least one state would always object to an increase in the power of Congress.

These weaknesses were quite evident during the early years of our nation. Congress was dependent upon the states for its money. If the states refused to pay their share of taxes, Congress could do absolutely nothing about it. Each state reserved to itself the right to put taxes on any goods that crossed its borders. The businessmen and the merchants complained loudly, but the central government did not have the power to help them. Conditions were not any better in our trade with foreign countries. Some states placed a tariff on goods that came from England; others permitted goods to enter their states tax free. This inconsistency caused a great deal of confusion.

The weakness led to more trouble in Massachusetts in 1786. A group of farmers from the western part of the state were in danger of losing their homes and farms because the state legislature had passed laws outlawing paper money. Led by Captain Daniel Shays, the farmers attacked the state arsenal at Springfield to capture the arms that they needed to carry on a fight against the state. The rebellion was finally put down by Massachusetts state troops, but throughout the trouble the central government was powerless to take any action.

Because boundaries of some of the states had not been drawn clearly, arguments arose between states. New York and New Hampshire both claimed the land that is now Vermont. Other states quarreled over the right to use rivers that flowed between them. Georgia and South Carolina, for example, argued over the Savannah River. Virginia and Maryland quarreled over the Potomac. Again, Congress was unable to settle such disputes because it lacked power.

Problems under the Articles of Confederation

Revision of the Articles. The dispute between Virginia and Maryland over navigation rights on the Potomac River led these two states to meet together in 1785 at Mount Vernon in an effort to try to settle their dispute. The delegates of these two states decided that other states, like Pennsylvania and Delaware, were also involved in the dispute. They also concluded that, since the question of commerce among the states concerned them all, they ought to invite all the states to send representatives to another conference.

The second conference, held at Annapolis in 1786, was attended by only five states—New York, New Jersey, Delaware, Pennsylvania, and Virginia. Alexander Hamilton of New York proposed that all the states be asked to send delegates to a new convention to meet at Philadelphia the next year. This convention would discuss not only commercial problems but also any suggestions to improve and to strengthen the government.

Congress approved the idea, and early in February of 1787, it recommended that the states send delegates to the Philadelphia convention for the express purpose of revising the Articles of Confederation. This was the convention that ultimately drafted the Constitution of the United States.

Achievement of the Articles. The Articles of Confederation lasted for only a few years (1781-89), but they did accomplish a number of important things. They served as the government that brought the Revolutionary War to a successful end. As a result, they not only won independence for the people of the United States but also established a favorable peace. They provided a framework of government that managed to keep the states together, even though the government had little power. Because they were weak, they pointed the way toward a better government. In spite of this weakness, they contributed some positive laws and were the basis of successful foreign relations.

Organization of western territories. Even before the Revolution, Americans had begun to cross the Appalachian Mountains. These pioneers wanted the government to admit the western lands to statehood. Congress, however, was slow to act, which caused many problems. For example, because both New York and New Hampshire contested Vermont's land claims, Vermont had to remain independent throughout the 1780s.

Finally, Congress passed two laws that helped bind the Western lands to the original thirteen colonies. The Land Ordinance of 1785 provided a solution for the problem of surveying and selling the land. Adopting New England's method of settlement by towns, Congress ordered the northwest divided into six-mile squares called townships.

Each township would contain 36 sections, and each section would contain 640 acres. Section 16 in the middle of each township was reserved for maintaining public schools, and the government retained three other sections for future use. The remainder was to be sold for a minimum of a dollar an acre. The minimum purchase was 640 acres or one section.

Congress had hoped to profit handsomely from the sale of its western empire, but it did not. Desperate for money, it turned to the quick sale of large tracts to speculators, who could then divide the lands and sell them at leisure—and at a handsome profit—to farmers. Before long, Congress was offering tracts of over 100,000 acres at pennies an acre to land companies that had ready cash.

Although the Ordinance of 1785 benefited eastern speculators at the expense of western farmers, it did have some advantages. The system avoided confusion over land ownership. Each plot of land in the west was precisely defined in terms of section and township. So useful was the system that it was later applied throughout the American West.

The second law, the Northwest Ordinance of 1787, provided government for the Northwest. Congress would appoint a governor and judges to preside over the territory initially. When the area had 5,000 males of voting age, it would be entitled to its own legislature and could send a nonvoting delegate to Congress. When it had 60,000 free inhabitants, the territory could be admitted to the Union as a state. The entire region between the Ohio River and the Great Lakes could eventually yield between three and five states. Ohio, Indiana, Illinois, Michigan, and Wisconsin eventually became states from this territory.

This ordinance, called the Northwest Ordinance, also included a bill of rights, granting freedom of speech and press, freedom of worship, and protection of judicial due process. In addition, the ordinance set down a policy of "utmost good faith" with regard to the Indians. Their lands and property were not to be taken from them without their consent, and all precautions were to be taken for "preventing wrongs being done to them, and for preserving peace and friendship with them." Unfortunately, this policy was largely ignored. Finally, Congress added to the ordinance a clause prohibiting slavery north of the Ohio River. It was the nation's first attempt to limit the spread of that economic institution.

The Northwest Ordinance provided the means for newly settled areas to enter the Union on an equal basis with the older states. The steps outlined by the ordinance, from wilderness to statehood, have been followed by every new state since 1787, including even the most recent admissions, Alaska and Hawaii.

Foreign relations. Congress made some attempts at establishing relationships with foreign nations but, for the most part, circumstances made success unlikely. It was very evident that England was not going to be friendly or was not reconciled to the loss of her empire. She held on to the fur-trading posts in land ceded to the United States. The reason given was that the colonists had not paid their debts to Loyalists whose lands were confiscated. However, it later appeared that England wanted to give the Canadian fur traders the opportunity to strengthen their ties with the Indians of the Northwest.

When America tried to restore trade relations with England, she passed laws restricting trade with America. England would not allow American goods to be imported, but she was ready to export her goods to America. This attitude hurt the American manufacturers.

It seemed that all of Europe was sitting back to see what would happen to the new country. Spain did not honor the terms of the Treaty of Paris but closed the port of New Orleans to American ships. This was a serious blow to western settlers because New Orleans was their chief outlet for commerce. Even France was cool in its treatment of the new nation. The time was not ripe for America to establish such relations, yet Congress did establish favorable trade relations with other European countries and with China.

Write the letter of the correct answer on the line.

3.14   One weakness of the Articles of Confederation was that they provided for _____
    a. weak Bill of Rights.
    b. a city-manager system.
    c. separate states with an appointed governor.
    d. amendment to laws only by a unanimous vote.

3.15   A rebellion of debt-ridden farmers was led by _____ .
    a. Patrick Henry
    b. Daniel Shays
    c. Daniel Webster
    d. Peter Zenger

3.16   Under the Articles of Confederation, Congress had no power to _____ .
    a. borrow money
    b. declare war
    c. collect taxes
    d. make treaties

3.17   The Articles of Confederation went into effect in _____ .
    a. 1776
    b. 1778
    c. 1781
    d. 1783

3.18   Under the Articles Of Confederation, the _____
    a. national government was superior to the states.
    b. states were superior to the national government.
    c. national government and the states were equal.

3.19   A serious dispute between the large and small states under the Articles was over the problem
        of _____ .
        a. control of the slave trade
        b. representation
        c. relations between the governors and the state legislatures
        d. who should vote

3.20   Ill feelings arose between the states because of claims to the _____ .
        a. Mississippi Valley
        b. Florida Territory
        c. Northwest Territory
        d. Louisiana Territory

3.21   The Northwest Ordinance of 1787 provided for the _____ .
        a. extension of slavery into the territories
        b. government of new territories
        c. extension of railroads in the west
        d. establishment of a military government

3.22   The Ordinance of 1785 _____
        a. benefited eastern speculators at the expense of western farmers.
        b. provided for the formation of five new states.
        c. protected the Indians from unlawful seizure of their lands.
        d. allowed Congress to levy taxes.

3.23   All of the following events were accomplishments of the Articles of Confederation except
        _____
        a. successful conclusion of the Revolutionary War.
        b. signing of the Treaty of Paris of 1783.
        c. passage of the Northwest Ordinance.
        d. adoption of the Declaration of Independence.

Fill in the blank.

3.24   Under the Land Ordinance of 1787, a territory could be admitted to the Union when it had
        _____ free inhabitants.

CONSTITUTION OF THE UNITED STATES

Eventually the Articles of Confederation were found insufficient to govern the United States. Alexander Hamilton warned in 1780, "The fundamental defect is a want of power in Congress. ...The idea of an uncontrollable sovereignty in each state...will defeat the other powers given to Congress, and make our union feeble and precarious." Many people agreed with him, and plans were made to create a stronger government.

THE
CONSTITUTIONS
OF THE SEVERAL
INDEPENDENT STATES
OF
AMERICA;
THE
DECLARATION OF INDEPENDENCE;
AND THE
ARTICLES OF CONFEDERATION
BETWEEN THE SAID STATES.

TO WHICH ARE NOW ADDED, THE
DECLARATION OF RIGHTS;
THE
NON-IMPORTATION AGREEMENT;
AND THE
PETITION OF CONGRESS TO THE KING
DELIVERED BY MR. PENN.

WITH AN
APPENDIX,
CONTAINING THE
TREATIES BETWEEN HIS MOST CHRISTAN MA-
JESTY AND THE UNITED STATES OF AMERICA;
THE
PROVISIONAL TREATY WITH AMERICA;
AND (*NEVER BEFORE PUBLISHED*)
AN AUTHENTIC COPY OF THE TREATY CON-
CLUDED BETWEEN THEIR HIGH MIGHTINES-
SES THE STATES-GENERAL, AND THE UNITED
STATES OF AMERICA.

THE WHOLE ARRANGED, WITH A
PREFACE AND DEDICATION,
By the Rev. WILLIAM JACKSON.

LONDON:
Printed for J. STOCKDALE, in Piccadilly. 1783.

The Constitutional Convention. In 1785 at a meeting called by George Washington to discuss a quarrel between Maryland and Virginia, James Madison proposed that representatives from each state meet to discuss common problems of commerce. He hoped that such a meeting would result in amendments to the Articles. However, only five states sent representatives to that meeting. At that time, another meeting was proposed, this one to be held in Philadelphia. Virginia endorsed the idea and chose George Washington to head its delegation. As other states agreed to be represented, Congress reluctantly gave its consent.

Among the famous Americans who attended the Constitutional Convention were George Washington, Benjamin Franklin, James Madison, Alexander Hamilton, and John Dickinson. Absent from this prestigious group were Thomas Jefferson, who was American minister in Paris, as well as Samuel Adams and Patrick Henry, who were the leading defenders of states' rights.

The first action of the convention was to elect George Washington as chairman. The second action was to vote to conduct all their sessions in private and to allow no news releases or reports of their progress. Madison later explained that the purpose of this decision was to encourage the delegates to vote as they believed they should, not because of any public commitment they might have made. By having no audience, the delegates might be more willing to change their minds as facts were presented.

The Virginia Plan. The delegate from Virginia, Edmund Randolph, was the first major speaker, and it was his proposal that led to the decision to draft a new document rather than amend the old one. He outlined the plan that the Virginia delegation wanted, which became known as the Virginia Plan.

Randolph proposed "that a national government ought to be established consisting of a supreme legislative, judiciary, and executive." The Virginians were aware that their plan exceeded the convention's authority to amend the Articles, but they apparently agreed with Washington's argument that the convention should not propose what it could not approve and that they had to propose what they believed was best, even if it was not within their power to change the situation.

Randolph's proposal to create a new government of three branches threw the convention into excited discussion. When the vote was finally taken, the convention agreed to establish a government consisting of three separate branches, creating a new framework of government rather than patching up the old Articles. The decision may well be considered the most important vote during the entire convention.

The New Jersey Plan. The Virginia Plan called for a Congress of two houses in which the total number of delegates would be divided among the states according to the free population of each state. Congress would have the power to select the executive and a system of national courts would be established.

Clearly, under the Virginia Plan the more heavily populated states would control Congress. Of course, the small states were opposed. Delegates from Connecticut, Maryland, Delaware, and New Jersey spoke out against the Virginia Plan. William Patterson of New Jersey presented an alternative plan based on the wishes of the small states. The New Jersey Plan called for a one-house legislature in which each state would cast only one vote, as in the Confederation Congress. Unlike the Articles of Confederation, however, the New Jersey Plan would allow Congress to regulate trade and to impose tariffs. It would provide for an executive council and a federal judiciary, but the powers of both would be restricted by Congress.

At this point the Convention reached a deadlock. Delegates furiously debated the two plans for two weeks. The heart of the quarrel was whether the central government would be given power to control the states. Under the Virginia Plan, where representation in Congress was based on population, it would have the power. Under the New Jersey Plan, which gave each state equal power regardless of population, it would not. The weather was hot and humid and tempers were short. Washington understood that further debate would not solve the problem. On July 2 he called for a vote on the New Jersey Plan. The result was a tie: five states for; five opposed. Georgia delegates were divided, New Hampshire was still not there, and Rhode Island was absent.

The "Great Compromise." At this crucial moment, the Convention agreed to submit the problem to a compromise committee of one delegate from each of the eleven participating states. The convention then adjourned for a few days while the committee worked on the problem.

When the convention reassembled, the compromise committee was ready to report. It suggested the creation of a two-house legislature composed of a House of Representatives and a Senate. To satisfy those who supported the Virginia Plan, members of the House were to be allotted to the states on the basis of population. The House members were to vote individually, not as part of a state delegation.

To satisfy followers of the New Jersey Plan, the states would have equal representation in the Senate. Each state would elect two senators, who would vote individually. The legislative authority of the two bodies was to be equal except that the House would originate all bills for raising revenue. This "Great Compromise," as it came to be called, was accepted by the convention on July 16.

The Three Branches. The delegates then turned to the question of the executive and judicial branches of the new government. Some delegates recommended that the executive branch be a committee rather than one individual. Some wanted the executive to serve for life; others, for one year only. Some thought Congress should appoint the executive. Others said the people should elect him. Finally, the delegates decided to entrust the executive powers to one man, to make his term of office four years, and to have him chosen by electors. These electors were to be selected by the states in whatever manner each of them chose. The electoral system proved to be one of the clumsiest parts of the Constitution.

Provision for federal courts was made; the judges were to be appointed by the President. Most of the delegates probably assumed that the courts system would be the weakest branch of government and that it would need to be protected from the other two branches.

Madison told the delegates that their real division of interest "did not lie between the large and small states, it lay between the northern and southern." The commercial North wanted a strong central government to control commerce, both interstate and foreign. The agricultural South wanted to be able to buy and sell in the most favorable market anywhere in the world. The South feared that Congress, under northern influence, might set up tariff duties that would block the free flow of goods to and from the country.

The delegates managed to find compromises that quieted these fears. Congress was given the power to regulate commerce among the states and with foreign nations, but specific limits on this power were adopted, which made southerners feel safer. Although Congress could not prevent the importation of slaves before 1808, it could levy a tax of ten dollars on each imported slave. Congress could not impose duties on exports, and two-thirds vote was needed in the Senate to ratify a treaty. Runaway or fugitive slaves were to be returned, even from free states, to their lawful masters.

By September of 1787, the convention had completed its outline for a new form of government. No delegate was satisfied with every part of the Constitution, but thirty-nine were willing to sign the document.

The final ratification. The Constitution became the leading topic of discussion throughout the new states. The convention provided that when nine state conventions ratified the Constitution it would go into effect in those states. Those who favored the Constitution became known as **Federalists**; opponents became known as **Antifederalists**. Most Federalists were willing to see the states surrender some of the power to the central government, but Antifederalists did not want the states to surrender any power to the central government.

The battle for **ratification** was hard fought. Had the Constitution been put to the test of popular vote in the fall of 1787, it would probably have been defeated. Many Americans feared that if it were adopted, the new government would destroy state sovereignty, a standing army would violate the freedom of citizens, taxes would be sharply increased, agricultural interests would be sacrificed to commercial interests, and individual liberties would be violated because the Constitution had no bill of rights. However, within a few months the Federalists dispelled these fears by using Washington's support of the Constitution and his willingness to serve as president if the document were ratified.

Alexander Hamilton, James Madison, and John Jay wrote a series of essays outlining the weaknesses of the Articles and the strengths of the Constitution. These articles were printed in many newspapers and in a book called *The Federalist*. Perhaps more than any other support, these essays swayed many votes in the ratifying conventions. Even today, these essays are one of the best interpretations of the Constitution and one of the most penetrating studies of government ever written.

Delaware, Pennsylvania, New Jersey, Connecticut, and Georgia were the first five states to ratify the Constitution. In Massachusetts ratification was uncertain until John Hancock threw his support to the Constitution. Then, by a narrow vote, Massachusetts ratified the Constitution. Maryland and South Carolina then joined the ranks. Finally, after a heated struggle, New Hampshire became the ninth state to ratify. The Constitution could go into effect in these nine states; but without the large states of New York and Virginia, many doubted if the new plan of government would succeed.

In Virginia the battle over ratification centered around Patrick Henry and George Mason, who were for states' rights, and James Madison, Edmund Randolph, and John Marshall, who supported the Constitution. Finally, when Virginia was promised that one of the first items of business would be a Bill of Rights, the Constitution was ratified by a narrow margin. Word was sent immediately to New York where the battle was still raging. Finally, fear of being excluded from the new government and word that Virginia had ratified influenced New York to become the eleventh state to ratify.

Constitution of the United States

The new form of government would now be tried. Preparations were made to elect a president, a vice president, and members of Congress. In 1789 the new government had actually taken over the reins of power when North Carolina decided to ratify. Not until 1790, however, did Rhode Island join the ranks of those who ratified the Constitution.

The federal system. The Constitution has met the test of time. To work out the Constitution, the Founding Fathers drew upon their knowledge of government histories and of government types that had worked and upon their own ideas about the needs of the American people.

One of the most difficult problems they faced was the distribution of power between the states and the central government. To solve this problem, they devised the Federal system, which provided a large measure of centralized control, yet preserved the benefits of state and local self-government. The central government received its powers from the people and would be answerable to the people for the way in which the powers were carried out.

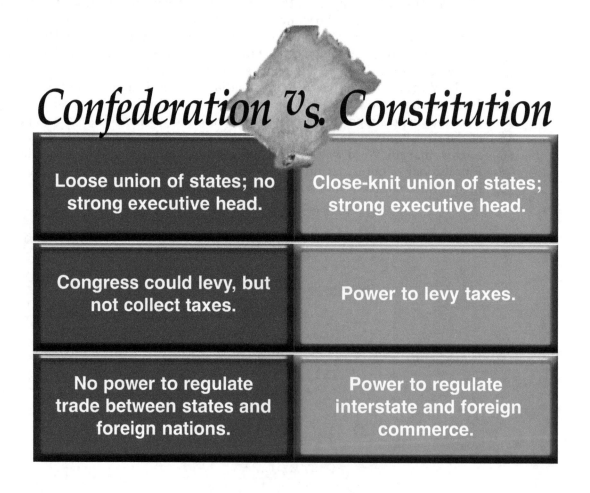

Confederation vs. Constitution

Loose union of states; no strong executive head.	Close-knit union of states; strong executive head.
Congress could levy, but not collect taxes.	Power to levy taxes.
No power to regulate trade between states and foreign nations.	Power to regulate interstate and foreign commerce.

Checks and balances. Another way in which the Constitution has proved successful is its system of checks and balances. When the founders provided for separate legislative, executive, and judicial branches, they made sure that no one branch of the government would get more than its share of power. Under the system established by the Constitutional Convention, the president can check Congress by vetoing legislation. The practice of judicial review has permitted the Supreme Court to check Congress by declaring laws unconstitutional.

Congress, on the other hand, can check both the president and members of the Court through its power to impeach government officials for "treason, bribery, or other high crimes and misdemeanors." Checks and balances were even set up within the legislative branch of government. Both houses of Congress, for example, have to approve a bill for it to become

52

law. This complicated system of checks and balances has prevented the concentration of political power in any one branch of the government. Some critics have contended that it leads to inefficiency and slows the process of government.

Flexible authority and power. Flexibility was also built into the Constitution by the delegates. Congress was given the authority to "make all laws which shall be necessary and proper for carrying into execution the foregoing powers." Congress and the Courts have interpreted this "necessary and proper" clause to meet the needs of the times. The "general welfare" clause is another source of flexibility in the Constitution. The amendment process adds flexibility to the Constitution.

Amending the Constitution. After ratification, Congress further increased the value of the Constitution by determining three ways in which it can be amended. First, an amendment may be proposed by two-thirds of both houses of Congress and ratified by the legislatures of three-fourths of the states. Second, it may be ratified by special conventions in three-fourths of the states. A third method is for an amendment to be proposed by a special convention called upon application by two-thirds of the state legislatures, and ratified by three-fourths of the state legislatures.

The Bill of Rights, the first ten amendments to the Constitution, is a safeguard of the rights of individuals. The amendments that compose the Bill of Rights were proposed by Congress in 1789 and went into effect in 1791. The document put together by the Constitutional Convention has remained the basis of the government of a great people for longer than any other single written document. It is indeed a tribute to the Fathers of the Constitution that the system of government they began has endured through the many startling changes that have taken place in this nation and in the world.

Bill Of Rights

Personal Security

Right to Own Property
Guarantee of Due Process of Law
No unwarranted Seizures or Searches
Guarantee of Just Compensation for Property

Bill Of Rights

Personal Liberties

Freedom of Religion
Freedom of Speech
Freedom of Assembly
Right of Petition

Bill Of Rights

Rights Of The Accused

Property Right to Trial by Jury
No Double Jeopardy
No Self-Incrimination
No Cruel or Unusual Punishments

Why were the sessions of the Constitutional Convention held secretly?

3.25 _____

_____

_____

_____

_____

Place a check beside the correct answers.

3.26 What is the system of checks and balances?

_____ a. Congress may override a veto with three-fourths vote.

_____ b. The President can veto legislation passed by Congress.

_____ c. The Supreme Court may override a veto by three-fourths vote.

_____ d. Congress may override a veto by two-thirds vote or impeach the President for misconduct.

_____ e. The President can only veto legislation passed by Congress with less than two-thirds vote in both houses.

_____ f. The Supreme Court may declare laws unconstitutional.

3.27 What are the three ways the Constitution can be amended?

_____ a. proposed by three-fourths of both houses and ratified by two-thirds of the states.

_____ b. proposed by two-thirds of both houses and ratified by three-fourths of the states.

_____ c. ratified by special conventions in three-fourths of the states.

_____ d. ratified by special conventions in one-half of the states.

_____ e. amendment called for special convention, called by two-thirds of state legislatures and ratified by three-fourths of state legislatures.

_____ f. amendment called for special convention, called by three-fourths of state legislatures and ratified by two-thirds of state legislatures.

Complete the following statement.

3.28 The group that favored the Constitution was called _____ , and those who opposed the Constitution were called _____ .

Write the letter of the correct answer on the line.

3.29   Why was the system of checks and balances included in the Constitution? _____
    a. to prevent one branch of the government from becoming too powerful
    b. to keep the President of the United States from vetoing legislation
    c. to slow down the process of government so it doesn't move too fast

Label the following columns Virginia Plan or New Jersey Plan.

3.30   _____ Plan: _____ Plan:
    three branches   three branches
    Congress: two houses   Congress: one house
    Representation by population   Representation by state
    Courts: national system   Courts: federal judiciary

Adult Check   _____
                   Initial   Date

Before you take this last Self Test, you may want to do one or more of these self checks.

1. ____ Read the objectives. Determine if you can do them.
2. ____ Restudy the material related to any objectives that you cannot do.
3. ____ Use the SQ3R study procedure to review the material:
        a. **S**can the sections.
        b. **Q**uestion yourself again (review the questions you wrote initially).
        c. **R**ead to answer your questions.
        d. **R**ecite the answers to yourself.
        e. **R**eview areas you didn't understand.
4. ____ Review all activities and Self Tests, writing a correct answer for each wrong answer.

SELF TEST 3

Answer *true* **or** *false* (each answer, 1 point).

3.01   _____   Many of the serious problems that plagued the government under the Articles of Confederation developed because of the limited power of the central government.

3.02   _____   The states of Ohio, Indiana, Michigan, Illinois, and Wisconsin were formed in the Northwest Territory.

3.03   _____   America's victory in the Revolutionary War was made more probable because of the aid provided by France.

3.04   _____   The Constitution provides for three branches of government: the executive, the legislative, and the judicial.

3.05   _____   The Intolerable Acts caused the formation of the Continental navy.

3.06   _____   Slavery was prohibited north of the Ohio River.

3.07   _____   Daniel Shay's rebellion united the colonies in recognizing a need for a strong national government.

3.08   _____   Nathan Hale gave his life for his country.

3.09   _____   After the Treaty of Paris, England was not friendly with the United States.

Complete the following statements (each answer, 2 points).

3.010   The number of Loyalists who left the United States after the Revolutionary War is estimated at _____ .

3.011   Proponents of the Constitution were called _____ .

3.012   Opponents of the Constitution were called _____ .

3.013   The Constitution Convention set up a system of _____ to prevent one branch from taking too much power.

3.014   The man who said "If this be treason, make the most of it" was _____ .

3.015   The Albany Plan of Union was proposed in order to strengthen the colonies against the _____ .

3.016   The first ten amendments to the Constitution that safeguard the rights of individuals are called the _____ .

3.017   The man credited with teaching the patriots how to fight professionally is _____ .

3.018   According to the Treaty of Paris of 1783, _____ would be open for trade to both the Americans and the _____ .

3.019   The author of *"Common Sense"* was _____ .

3.020   The _____ Acts were created to punish _____ for its infamous Tea Party.

Place a check on the lines of the correct answers (each lettered blank, 1 points).

3.021   Select four weaknesses of the Articles of Confederation.

_____   a. They could not contribute any positive laws to the government.

_____   b. They served as the government that brought on the Revolutionary War.

_____   c. Congress had no power to collect taxes.

_____   d. Equal voting power in Congress led to jealousies between states.

_____   e. Congress had no power to levy taxes.

_____   f. Congress had no power to control trade.

_____   g. There was no system of national courts.

_____   h. There was no voting power for small states.

3.022   A political democracy needs a strong social foundation if it is to survive. Which three of the following changes helped develop a strong social foundation after the Revolution?

_____   a. separation of church and state

_____   b. small farmers had opportunity to buy land

_____   c. steps were taken to emancipate slaves

_____   d. state governments were established

_____   e. public education became common

Write the letter of the correct answer on the line (each answer, 2 points).

3.023   The Northwest Ordinance of 1787 provided for the _____ .
   a. extension of slavery into the territories
   b. government of new territories
   c. extension of railroads in the west
   d. establishment of a military government

3.024   Which was not a feature of the new state governments? _____
   a. broad legislative powers
   b. tight control over taxation
   c. unlimited governmental powers
   d. qualifications for office-holders and voters

42 / 52

Score
Adult Check   _____
                   _____
                   Initial   Date

Before you take the LIFEPAC Test, you may want to do one or more of these self checks.

1. _____ Read the objectives. Determine if you can do them.
2. _____ Restudy the material related to any objectives that you cannot do.
3. _____ Use the SQ3R study procedure to review the material.
4. _____ Review all activities and Self Tests, and LIFEPAC Glossary.
5. _____ Restudy areas of weakness indicated by the last Self Test.